All Things Restored

Praise for All Things Restored

"It is a great joy to see the leadership and faithfulness of Pastor Sebastiaan Van Wessem. His steadfast commitment to the Kingdom of God, his love for Israel and the Jewish people, and his pursuit of biblical truth that brings believers into maturity are both rare and refreshing in our day. Pastor Sebastiaan carries the heart of a true shepherd – one who teaches not for applause, but to raise a people who walk in the fullness of God's purposes. How inspiring to witness an international Christian leader in Europe and the nations taking up this torch – proclaiming God's promises, standing with Israel, and preparing the Bride for her soon-coming King."

Paul Wilbur
Worship leader, author and founder of Wilbur Ministries

"Few messages resonate more deeply with the human heart than the hope of what the Bible calls, 'the restoration of all things.' In a time when much of the Church has lost sight of the story that holds all things together, this work calls us back to the heartbeat of God's redemptive plan. I'm grateful that Pastor Sebastiaan has written this; its message is not only vital, but timely and much needed in the Church today."

Joel Richardson
NYT bestselling author, teacher, and craftsman.

"Sebastiaan van Wessem has written a very profound work of theology. It presents a more adequate overall narrative on the story of Biblical redemption and restoration. It is in accord with other recent scholarly works and is very well documented in many sources. It is, in my view, a foundational work."

Daniel Juster, Th.D.
Founding president of the Union of Messianic Jewish Congregations
and Tikkun International

"It's indeed an honor for me to write an endorsement for Sebastiaan's book. Sebastiaan is a brother who has been instrumental in the past. He has worked with our mission teams, both those based in Europe and those who travel from Africa to Europe occasionally. I find his book All Things Restored quite fascinating. It's not only timely but also prophetic. It explains a lot of mysteries that, when placed together, paint a glorious picture of God's purposes and plans. I love the way Sebastiaan threads the story of God's plans and purposes right from Eden, through the birth of Israel as a nation, through the many lessons we learn from Israel's journey, and ultimately to the birth of the church. Indeed, everything is shown to be restorative. But even in this present age, the church has been rocked by antisemitism and replacement theology. I see this book as God's intervention to take us back to the place of restoration and to be one new man in Christ. Finally, the book paints a clear path forward and shows how we should prepare for the return of our Lord Jesus and the dawn of eternity. This is a must-read, and I fully recommend it to anyone who is hungry for God's plans."

Dr. John W. Mulinde
Founder and Global Overseer of World Trumpet Mission
Kampala, Uganda

"In All Things Restored, Pastor Sebastiaan van Wessem offers a timely and thoughtful invitation for the global Church to rediscover the fullness of God's redemptive story. His emphasis on unity, holiness, and the coming restoration of all things reflects the heart of the gospel and the hope of Jesus' return. While this book approaches certain themes through a distinct theological lens, its call for humility, reconciliation, and renewed devotion to Christ is one that transcends boundaries and blesses the entire Body of Christ."

Tim Timberlake
Senior pastor (Celebration Church of Jacksonville, Florida)
Author of The Bumpy Road to Better

"This remarkable work of pastor Sebastiaan van Wessem on the theme of 'all things restored' offers a profound and unifying vision which is drawing deeply from both Jewish and Christian theology. It bridges historical divides and illuminates the shared hope of divine restoration woven throughout the Scriptures. A timely inspiring contribution for scholars and seekers alike."

Samuel Kidane
Director of Ethiopian Messianic Jewish Alliance

"Do you wonder how to make sense of the raging debates over Jews and Israel in the Bible and how they relate to Jesus and the gospel? This elegant study, irenic in its treatment of clashing convictions, traces the story of restoration from Genesis to Revelation. It is attentive to the work of esteemed scholars and the plain sense of the biblical text. Every serious Christian should read it."

Gerald McDermott, Ph.D.
Author of Israel Matters and A New History of Redemption
Distinguished professor of theology at Jerusalem Seminary and Reformed Episcopal Seminary

"Sebastiaan van Wessem weaves together Israel's story, the Church's calling, and the Kingdom's hope into one redemptive thread. All Things Restored is a deeply biblical work that awakens faith in God's promise to make all things new and brings coherence to the unfolding story of the Lord's restoration of the nations. This book paves the way for a transformative journey for every follower of Jesus."

Simon Hemsley
Lead pastor (His Church in Durban, South Africa)

"This is a well-researched, written and articulated narration of God's Kingdom. Pastor Sebastiaan has presented, with clarity and simplicity the eternal message of hope and the new creation for the growth and strengthening of the believer! This is a great resource for the Church and a must read for everyone!"

Dixon Changara
Lead Pastor (Celebration Church of Zimbabwe)

"All Things Restored is a compelling invitation for the Church to rekindle its hope in the age to come. Sebastiaan van Wessem writes with theological depth, helping readers see the redemptive plan God has been telling us since the beginning. This book will awaken your faith and set your gaze firmly on the mission of Jesus. I wholeheartedly recommend it."

Stacy Henagan
Senior pastor (KeyPoint Church in Arkansas) and
author of Breathe Again

All Things Restored

A Story of Kingdom, Hope, and New Creation

Sebastiaan van Wessem

KNGDMPRESS

KNGDM Press

An imprint of Global Kingdom Alliance, Inc.

Jacksonville, Florida (United States of America)

KNGDM Press is the publishing imprint of Global Kingdom Alliance, Inc., operating publicly as KNGDM Alliance. We exist to resource the global Body of Messiah with biblically faithful, restoration-oriented teaching rooted in the Gospel of the Kingdom. Through books and other ministry tools, we equip Messianic Jewish and Gentile believers to unite as "one new humanity under Messiah," honor the covenant promises toward Israel and the nations, and carry God's Kingdom message to all tribes and tongues worldwide.

Our aim is to advance the vision of KNGDM Alliance: a vibrant, apostolically led global family of congregations, ministries, and leaders committed to worship, prayer, sound teaching, and bringing in a Kingdom harvest.

KNGDMPRESS

www.kngdmpress.com

All Things Restored – KNGDM Press, 2026

Published by KNGDM Press
An imprint of Global Kingdom Alliance, Inc. (operating publicly as KNGDM Alliance)
Printed and distributed worldwide through print-on-demand services.

Scripture quotations, unless otherwise indicated, are from the *ESV*® *Bible (The Holy Bible, English Standard Version`)*, © 2001 by Crossway, a publishing ministry of Good News Publishers. ESV Text Edition: 2025. Used by permission. All rights reserved.

ISBN: 979-8-9940742-0-6

Library of Congress Control Number: 2026900920

Cover design and interior design by Levi Toledo

All Things Restored — KNGDM Press, 2026

To my twin sons, Miles and William –
may you grow to love the story of Scripture,
walk in the ways of the King,
and live as signs of his coming restoration.

Table of Contents

Preface

Writing this book has been both a theological and a deeply personal journey. Many people have played a part in it – through encouragement, insight, or simply patience.

To my wife Eva, whose interest in this project grew along the way, and who graciously put up with the many hours I spent writing, revising, and thinking aloud at odd moments. Thank you for your love, your patience, your understanding and your encouragement throughout this long process.

To Paul and Nate Wilbur, and to Simon Hemsley, whose friendship and spiritual insight were instrumental in the relaunch of what is now KNGDM Alliance. Their passion for reconciliation between Jewish and Gentile believers has profoundly shaped my own journey and helped anchor this movement in the story of God's restoration.

To Mario van Keulen, who worked tirelessly with me through the manuscript – reading, refining, and helping give structure and prophetic clarity to the ideas on these pages. Your friendship and wisdom have shaped this work in more ways than I can count.

To Daniel Juster and Gerald McDermott, for your encouragement along the way. Your confidence in my theological direction and your example as scholars helped me believe that this project was worth pursuing.

To all the friends, pastors, and colleagues who told me over the years – often after listening to my theological ramblings – "You really should write a book." I was slow to listen but, in the end, I did!

A special word of thanks goes to my Celebration Church Netherlands family, and to all those in the KNGDM Alliance network who graciously became the first hearers of many of these ideas. You were my testing ground, conversation partners, and encouragers as the theology of this book began to take shape. Your faith, hunger for truth, and shared love for God's Kingdom inspired me to keep writing.

This book was born out of a desire to help readers see the Bible as one great, unfolding story of restoration. When we read Scripture within its true contexts – historical, cultural, and covenantal – we discover a unified narrative revealing God's faithfulness to Israel, to the nations, and to creation itself. I hope that this work will open eyes to the beauty of that story and renew hearts with the hope of all things restored.

— *Sebastiaan van Wessem*
Almere, The Netherlands

Introduction

I never thought I would sit down to write a book. I've always been the sort of person who gets distracted too easily for such a long project. Yet an idea kept stirring in my heart: the networks I lead and relate to around the world could use a clear and accessible book that lays out the framework of Restorationism – or restorationist theology – in one place.

A Revival and the Fallout

Since 2018, I've been on a journey of reconstruction – not deconstruction – of my Christian faith. Until then, I was deeply invested in the church-growth movement as a local pastor in Hilversum, the Netherlands. My focus was on making the church as seeker-friendly as possible, drawing as many people in as we could. It was a fruitful season, at least on the surface: many people came through the doors of our historic building, responded to altar calls, and were baptized. God moved powerfully. And yet, something still felt missing.

At times, while preaching or leading an altar call, I would hear myself saying things and wonder whether I still believed them in the way I once did. I never doubted the core truths of the faith, but I began to question how closely our expression of Christianity resembled the faith the apostles preached and practiced.

That same year, a revival broke out in one of the congregations in our network. It shook my theology. I began reading scholars who approached the Scriptures in their Ancient Near Eastern context. Around the same time, I developed friendships in Messianic Jewish circles. I began rethinking my views on the Sabbath, the biblical feasts, the *Torah*, and, most importantly, the Jewishness of Jesus.

In 2022, this revival came to an abrupt halt, and a Christian network that had emerged from it fell apart. I felt responsible for pastoring the relational network of leaders that remained. Two close friends from that network, Messianic Jewish worship leader Paul Wilbur and his son Nate, encouraged me to continue. I sensed the Lord drawing our focus toward Jerusalem, without yet understanding its prophetic significance.

"Who Do We Know in Jerusalem?"

I asked them the question: "Who do we know in Jerusalem?" That simple question set a new trajectory in motion. It led to a Zoom call in August 2022 with Asher Intrater and Ariel Blumenthal of Tikkun Global. I still remember the unstable internet connection from the Christian campsite in the east of my country. Three months later, my friend Pastor Simon Hemsley from Durban, South Africa, and I traveled to Jerusalem to meet our new Israeli friends in person. That trip changed me.

I discovered that leaders in the modern Messianic Jewish movement often read the Scriptures with a simplicity and clarity that arise from knowing the *Torah* and the prophets intimately, free from many of the Western theological filters through which I had been trained to read the Bible. I came to realize that many theologians and pastors around the world share a similar theological perspective. I noticed some of them coined the term "Restorationism," drawn from Acts 3:21: "Heaven must take Him in until the time comes for the restoration of all things, which God announced long ago through His holy prophets" (BSB). This echoes the disciples' question after forty days of intense Kingdom teaching following Jesus' resurrection: "Lord, will you at this time restore the kingdom to Israel?" (Acts 1:6). Jesus did not rebuke their expectation. He only corrected their sense of timing. The timing was for the Father to decide. Their focus had to be on the mission Jesus gave them, one that stretched far beyond the borders of a restored Kingdom of Israel – even to the ends of the earth (Acts 1:7-8).[1]

What is Restorationism?

Restorationism is the conviction that God's redemptive plan includes the renewal of both Israel and the Church, culminating in the return of Jesus and the final restoration of all things. It affirms God's enduring covenant with Israel – including the Jewish people's physical return to their land and spiritual renewal through faith in Messiah – while envisioning the Church restored to its apostolic roots of faith, unity, and power. Central to this vision is the "one new man" (Eph. 2:15): a reconciled Body of Jewish and Gentile believers, through whom God will reveal his glory in the last days.

This book is my attempt to spell out that vision clearly – for pastors, church leaders, scholars, as well as believers who want to take a deeper dive in Scripture. My hope is to build a bridge between Messianic Jewish and Gentile believers, and to spark further theological reflection and debate on this vital theme.

How is "Our" Restorationism Different?

The Restorationism explored in this book stands apart from earlier movements that have carried the same name. In church history, "Restorationism" has described various groups – especially in the nineteenth and early twentieth centuries – that sought to recreate the form and practices of

---

1   I always thought that Jesus corrected the disciples' Kingdom expectations. I thought that the Kingdom would be more of a spiritual kingdom, and not a physical kingdom. But notice how Jesus here doesn't correct the disciples' expectations, just their sense of timing. Also, notice that Jesus in 40 days of in-depth training would not have left any questions about what the Kingdom would look like unanswered. The idea of the "restoration of all things" is a thoroughly Jewish concept, also referred to as *tikkun olam* – the mending of the world. God will mend the world when his Kingdom here on earth will come to its consummation.

the early Church. Movements such as Stone-Campbell (Disciples of Christ, Churches of Christ), the Christadelphians, Latter-day Saints (Mormons), Jehovah's Witnesses, and others aimed to restore primitive Christianity after centuries of decline, often rejecting creeds, traditions, and denominational structures, and sometimes claiming exclusive authenticity.

The Restorationism presented here moves in a different direction. It is not confined by ethnicity, denomination, nostalgia, or sectarianism. Rather than reconstructing an ancient model, it represents a theological vision shared by many followers of Jesus, Jewish and non-Jewish alike, who long to see God's promises to Israel and the global Church fulfilled in harmony with the full witness of Scripture. It seeks to recover Christianity's Jewish roots and the unified story of the Old and New Testaments, long obscured by later interpretations.

This restoration is holistic. It affirms God's enduring covenant with Israel, the regathering and renewal of the Jewish people, the revitalization of the worldwide Church on apostolic foundations, and the reconciliation of Jew and Gentile in Messiah as "one new man" (Eph. 2:15). At its heart, it is a vision of unity in diversity, filled with hope and expectation for the day when the King returns and the world is made whole.

The Restorationism we present is not about nostalgia or exclusivity but about a living and biblical hope of restoration. It is the conviction that God's purposes for Israel and the nations are once again converging in our day – signs of a divine story coming full circle. As the Church is being restored to her apostolic foundations and Israel is being awakened to her covenant destiny, both point toward the same glorious horizon: the final restoration of all things at the return of Jesus.

"Heaven must take Him in
until the time comes
for the restoration of all things,
which God announced long ago
through His holy prophets."
(Acts 3:21 BSB).

Chapter 1

The Creator's Purpose:
Eden as the Prototype of Restoration

The Bible is much more than a collection of doctrines, laws, or moral tales. It is a unified story, a drama that begins in perfect harmony, is shattered by rebellion, and then moves relentlessly toward complete restoration. This story shapes everything: the way we see God, the way we see ourselves, and the way we see our mission in the world.

From Genesis to Revelation, Scripture traces a clear arc: creation, rebellion, redemption, and renewal. The story does not begin in a vacuum but in the beauty and order of a sacred garden called Eden. This first scene sets the trajectory of the entire biblical narrative. Eden is not simply "paradise lost." It is the blueprint of God's intent, the prototype of his Kingdom, and the destination toward which the story of redemption is headed.

Seeing the Bible as a single, coherent story is essential. Many modern readers approach it as a set of disconnected parts: laws here, promises there, moral examples scattered in between. But the ancient authors wrote within a narrative framework rooted in God's ongoing covenant dealings with creation and his people. Understanding this storyline helps us avoid reading isolated fragments and instead see the unbroken flow of God's purposes.

In this light, Eden is not just the beginning. It is also the goal. The entire history of redemption can be viewed as the story of God restoring his dwelling place with humanity in a temple-like new creation. That theme of restoration is the golden thread running through the Law and Prophets, the ministry of Jesus, the apostolic witness, and the prophetic visions of Revelation. From the first page to the last, the Bible ties the renewal of the world to the restoration of God's presence among his people.

Seeing Scripture this way changes how we think about salvation and mission. The gospel is not an evacuation plan from creation but a rescue plan for creation. Our hope is not in an escape from this world but in the renewal of the world. Peter calls this "the restoration of all things" (Acts 3:21). To understand that restoration, we must return to where the story began: Eden, God's first dwelling with humanity.

Eden as Temple and Sanctuary

Eden was not an ordinary garden. It was the first sacred space, the original meeting point of heaven and earth, where YHWH's presence rested and his divine council gathered.[2] The biblical author describes Eden with imagery that is later echoed in Israel's tabernacle and temple. God "walks" in the garden (Gen.3:8), just as he "walks" in the tabernacle (Lev. 26:12). Eden's entrance faces east, just like the tabernacle's entrance (Gen. 3:24; cf. Ezek. 43:1-4). Cherubim are stationed as guardians in both places (Gen. 3:24; Ex. 25:18-22). These parallels are intentional. From the very beginning, the Bible uses temple language to show that God's dwelling with humanity is a central theme.

---

2 Michael S. Heiser, *The Unseen Realm: Recovering the Supernatural Worldview of the Bible* (Bellingham, WA: Lexham Press, 2015), 44-48. Heiser's book builds a compelling case for lower *elohim* (spiritual beings) who are created by YHWH who serve with him on a divine council. A great example is Psalm 82, but there are many other passages in the Hebrew Bible that support this idea. I often use YHWH in this book instead of "God" or "the Lord." YHWH is the transliteration of the Hebrew letters yod-hay-vav-hay in the Old Testament, which is the covenant name of God. Since according to Jewish tradition no one knows how to pronounce this name, I will refrain from using vowels and stick to what the Biblical text presents us. YHWH is also called the "*Tetragrammaton*" (Greek for "four letters").

Gordon Wenham observes, "The garden of Eden is not viewed by the author of Genesis simply as a piece of Mesopotamian farmland, but as an archetypal sanctuary – a place where God dwells and where man should worship him."[3] Michael Heiser adds, "Eden was God's home on earth. It was his residence. And where the King lives, his [divine] council meets."[4] That means Eden is both the first temple and the pattern for every sanctuary to come.

In the ancient world, temples were often located on high ground to symbolize proximity to the gods.[5] Many Jewish and Christian traditions connect Eden with a mountain, specifically Mount Moriah, later known as Mount Zion, which is the Temple Mount in Jerusalem. The prophet Ezekiel links the images directly, describing Eden as "the garden of God" and "the holy mountain of God" (Ezek. 28:13-14). Ancient traditions from the Second Temple and early rabbinic era, such as *Pirkei DeRabbi Eliezer*, even place Eden at the very site where the Jerusalem temple would one day stand, underscoring the continuity between God's original habitation and his chosen place of worship.[6]

---

3   Gordon J. Wenham, "Sanctuary Symbolism in the Garden of Eden Story," in *Proceedings of the Ninth World Congress of Jewish Studies* (Jerusalem: World Union of Jewish Studies, 1986), 19.

4   Heiser, *The Unseen Realm*, 44.

5   L. Michael Morales, *The Tabernacle Pre-Figured: Cosmic Mountain Ideology in Genesis and Exodus*, A dissertation submitted in completion of requirements for the degree Doctor of Philosophy, University of Bristol / Trinity College, 9 May 2011, p.2.

6   Pirkei DeRabbi Eliezer, trans. Gerald Friedlander (London, 1916), ch. 12, https://www.sefaria.org/Pirkei_DeRabbi_Eliezer.12.1, accessed on July 8, 2025. This early rabbinic midrash retells and expands the biblical narrative from Genesis through Numbers, including ethical teachings, ancient Jewish customs, legends, and calculations concerning creation and the end of days. Traditionally attributed to Rabbi Eliezer ben Hyrcanus, a 2nd-century sage, it was likely edited in the 8th or 9th century. In 12:1 it reads: "With love abounding did the Holy One, blessed be he, love the first man, inasmuch as he created him in a pure locality, in the place of the Temple, and he brought him into his palace, as it is said, 'And the LORD God took the man, and put him into the Garden of Eden to dress it and to keep it' (Gen 2:15)...."

This "sacred geography" unites Eden and Zion into a single redemptive storyline: from the first garden-temple, through Israel's sanctuary, to the New Jerusalem (Isa. 2:2-4; Rev. 21:10). Even the rivers of Genesis 2 hint at this connection. One, the Gihon, has been identified by some ancient interpreters with Jerusalem's Gihon Spring, the city's ancient water source and a vital part of its temple rituals. Whether the geographical identification is precise or not, the symbolism is powerful: temple, spring, and mountain all come together as enduring images of God's life-giving presence.[7]

Eden, then, is not just the backdrop for humanity's beginning. It is the archetype of where creation is heading. Jerusalem stands as a prophetic echo of Eden, and points to the New Jerusalem where its consummation will be – a restored sacred city where God dwells with his people forever.

Humanity's Priestly Calling and the Image of God

In the very beginning, humanity was created in the image of God (*tselem elohim*, Gen. 1:26-28) and entrusted with dominion over creation. This dominion was never intended as domination. It is sacred stewardship, a partnership with God in caring for what he has made. Genesis describes humanity's vocation using priestly language: "to cultivate it and keep it" (Gen. 2:15 BSB). As G.K. Beale notes, the Hebrew verbs used here, *'abad* ("serve") and *šāmar* ("guard"), commonly refer to priestly duties in Israel's sanctuary, so the author of Genesis has sacred service in mind, not just agricultural labor (Num. 3:7-8; 18:5-6).[8] Humanity's task in

---

7   Stephen L. Cook, "The Temple in the Christian Bible," *St Andrews Encyclopaedia of Theology* (Aug. 2023), https://www.saet.ac.uk/Christianity/TheTempleintheChristianBible (accessed on 21 Nov. 2025).

8   Beale, *A New Testament Biblical Theology* (Grand Rapids, MI: Baker Academic, 2011), 617-618.

Eden, then, was to be royal priests: representatives of God's rule and caretakers of his temple-garden.

This priestly vocation reaches deeper than mere responsibility. In the ancient Near East, kings were often described as "images" of the gods, mediating the authority of the gods on earth. But Genesis democratizes this dignity: every human being, not just the elites, is called to image the God who created the universe, share his kingship, and reflect his character. As Michael Heiser writes, "We are God's representatives on earth. To be human is to image God."[9] We are God's representatives – his earthly council and administration. To bear God's image is to actively participate in his purpose for creation.

Carmen Joy Imes takes this further by arguing that bearing God's image includes bearing his name, which is a call to represent him relationally and ethically, to carry his reputation and character into the world. This priestly identity is not just about status. It is about vocation. Human beings are meant to be visible reminders of who God is – living as ambassadors, mediators, and witnesses to his justice, mercy, and holiness.[10]

This original purpose undergirds the whole biblical story. Sin distorts the image but redemption in Messiah restores it. In Jesus, humanity's priestly calling is renewed, not just so that we could be saved individually but that our whole vocation of worship, stewardship, and witness can be restored (Rev. 21:22-27). The priesthood of all believers now means every follower of Jesus is called to take part in *tikkun olam* – repairing and restoring the world by extending God's mercy, pursuing justice, and manifesting

---

9   Heiser, *The Unseen Realm*, 43.

10   Carmen Joy Imes, *Bearing Yhwh's Name at Sinai - A Reexamination of the Name Command of the Decalogue* (University Park, PA: Eisenbrauns, 2018), 178-179.

his presence.[11] Our participation in God's mission is not peripheral but central. We are called to help creation reflect the character and rule of its Creator (Micah 6:8).[12]

Becoming Part of God's Family

To be created in God's image is, at its core, to be welcomed into his family. From the opening chapters of Genesis throughout the whole Bible the relationship between the Creator and humanity is framed in terms of kinship: God as Father, humanity as his children (Luke 3:38). Just as children resemble their parents in appearance and character, human beings were meant to reflect their Father's likeness and ways, both in who they are and in what they do.

This family identity is not static. It comes with a calling. To be a child of God is to take part in the "family business": tending, governing, and blessing the earth under his authority. Michael Heiser describes Adam and Eve as "Yahweh's choice to be steward-kings over a global Eden under his authority,"[13] a role that combines both royal responsibility and intimate relationship. Eden, therefore, stands as the prototype of a family-Kingdom: God's dwelling with his people, his reign mediated through his sons and daughters, and his presence filling creation.

The story of Scripture continually returns to this theme of divine family. Israel is called God's "firstborn son" (Exod. 4:22; cf. Eph. 2:19),

---

11 Anna Beth Havenar, "Repairing a Broken World: The Jewish Concept of Tikkun Olam," *Light of Messiah Ministries Blog*, 6 Feb. 2024, https://lightofmessiah.org/blog/repairing-a-broken-world-the-jewish-concept-of-tikkun-olam (accessed on 21 Nov. 2025).

12 In Jewish thought, especially within Second Temple Judaism and later rabbinic tradition, *tikkun olam* captures the idea that God's people are called to participate actively in healing and restoring all aspects of creation, with the goal to bring about social justice, righteousness, and peace. It's a holistic mission that goes beyond personal spirituality to include restoration of relationships and society.

13 Heiser, *The Unseen Realm*, 56.

chosen to reflect his character to the nations. In the New Testament, believers, both Jews and Gentiles, are adopted into God's household through Messiah Jesus, "the firstborn among many brothers" (Rom. 8:29; Gal. 4:4-7). Through union with him, the family Adam was meant to begin is finally restored and expanded.

This identity also transforms our posture in God's mission. We are not distant subjects serving an impersonal ruler, but sons and daughters representing our Father's interests in the world. We are his ambassadors (2 Cor. 5:20). Our stewardship is relational, rooted in trust, love, and shared purpose, not in fear or compulsion. As members of God's royal household, we bear his name and extend his blessings to the nations, anticipating the day when this reality reaches its fullness in the new creation, "when... the dwelling place of God is with man" (Rev. 21:3).

Exile from Eden: The First Rift

The narrative of Genesis quickly turns from intimate communion to a tragic disruption. The Fall (Gen. 3) damaged God's original order, and the consequences reached every corner of creation. Yet this moment of rebellion is not an isolated event. Scripture traces a trilogy of primeval rebellions: humanity's disobedience in Eden (Gen. 3), the corruption that brings the flood in Noah's day (Gen.6:1-4), and the idolatrous unity at Babel (Gen. 11:1-9). Each episode deepens the separation between God and humanity, marking a pattern of exile and alienation.

Adam and Eve's expulsion from the garden (Gen. 3:23-24) was far more than a change of location. It marked the loss of access to God's presence, the loss of humanity's priestly vocation, and the beginning of a deep rift within creation itself. Where humans had once enjoyed direct fellowship with God as royal priests, they were now driven east of Eden, exiled and longing for the restoration of all that had been lost.[14]

The exile motif becomes a central theme in the biblical story.[15] We will see it again when Israel is expelled from the Promised Land. The theme of exile is used as a symbol for all kinds of alienation: spiritual, relational, and societal. Sin not only drives a wedge in the relationship between God and humanity but also breaks their relationships with one another and with creation. Paul describes this state as a life under the "domain of darkness" (Col. 1:13). The image of God in humanity is marred, and the mission to serve and reflect him is disrupted, leaving creation fractured and incomplete, longing for its renewal (Rom. 8:19-21).[16] Yet even in exile, the promise of restoration begins to take root. The biblical drama now turns toward the hope that God will not abandon his family but will make a way for them back home.

The Restoration Theme Begins

Even in the midst of judgment, God plants a seed of hope. In Genesis 3:15, often called the *protoevangelium* ("first gospel"), God speaks of ongoing conflict between the serpent and the woman, and between their offspring: "he shall bruise your head, and you shall bruise his heel." This promise, though brief and

---

14   The Bible states that after the fall, humanity moved east of Eden in Genesis 3:24: "So he drove out the man, and at the east of the garden of Eden he placed the cherubim and a flaming sword that turned every way to guard the way to the tree of life." Additionally, after Cain killed Abel, we read in Genesis 4:16: "Then Cain went away from the presence of the Lord and settled in the land of Nod, east of Eden."

15   Bryan D. Estelle, "The Exodus Motif in the Christian Bible," *St Andrews Encyclopaedia of Theology*, https://www.saet.ac.uk/Christianity/TheExodusMotifintheChristianBible (accessed on 21 Nov. 2025).

16   See Beale, *A New Testament Biblical Theology*, 384. Beale explains that after the fall, Adam and Eve were no longer able to fulfill humanity's original mandate to reflect God's image and fill the earth with his glory; rather, their efforts became frustrated and marked by sorrow, signaling a loss of their intended vocation.

cryptic in its original setting, becomes the seedbed for the Bible's restoration story.[17]

To ancient Israel and to the early Church, this verse signaled more than a clash of good and evil. It pointed to a final victory. The serpent, emblem of rebellion, would one day be crushed. Many Christian interpreters, from the Church Fathers to modern scholars, have understood the "seed of the woman" as a prophetic anticipation of Messiah, the one who would undo the damage of Eden, defeat the adversary, and restore creation to its intended harmony.[18]

This promise is important not just because it predicts victory but because it is the first hint of hope that runs through the whole Bible. Later prophetic passages pick up the theme: the son of David who will rule in righteousness (Isa. 9:6-7), the servant who will bring healing and justice to the nations (Isa. 42:1-9), the King whose reign will reverse the curse and bring peace even to creation itself (Isa. 11:1-9). The New Testament writers see these threads converging in Jesus, whose life, death, and resurrection begin the ultimate reversal of the tragedy of Eden and the other two primeval rebellions.

From this moment forward, the Bible's narrative is set on a trajectory toward restoration. The exile from Eden will not be the final word: a Deliverer is promised, the enemy will be defeated, and the presence of God will once again dwell with his people.

---

17 C. John Collins, *Genesis 1-4: A Linguistic, Literary, and Theological Commentary* (Phillipsburg, NJ: P&R Publishing, 2006), 155-159, 176-178.

18 Kevin S. Chen, *The Messianic Vision of the Pentateuch: A Biblical-Theological Introduction to the Messiah and His People* (Downers Grove, IL: IVP Academic, 2019), ch.1.

Pastoral Reflection: Eden, Identity, and the Church Today

Why does the story of Eden matter for pastors and leaders today? Eden provides three essential anchors: identity, mission, and hope. First, Eden reframes our identity; it reveals who we truly are. We are not only defined as sinners in need of rescue but as image-bearers called to live as royal priests, destined to reign in Jesus' name with his delegated authority (Rom. 5:17). When the Church understands itself in light of God's original design rather than merely as exiles from Eden, it changes how we teach, disciple, and lead. Our message is not only about escape from sin but about a restoration to our true identity and calling.

Second, Eden redefines our mission. The gospel is not simply about getting people into heaven but about forming a community that reflects God's presence and reign on earth. The New Testament pictures the Church as a mobile temple, a "garden-people" whose life brings healing, justice, and fruitfulness wherever they go (Rev. 22:2). So, pastors should encourage their congregations to take an active, visible part in God's work of renewing the world through worship, discipleship, and shared life together.

Finally, Eden gives us hope. Restoration is not wishful thinking – it is the heartbeat of Scripture. God's purpose is to renew all things under the reign of Messiah. Our ministry is not merely to lead individuals to salvation but to join him in the renewal of reality itself: families, neighborhoods, creation, and ultimately the whole world. The story is not over, and our calling carries far more dignity and hope than we often realize. Every act of faithfulness, every work of love, every glimpse of beauty is a foretaste of the world to come: the beginning of Eden restored.

"Behold, the dwelling place
of God is with man.
He will dwell with them,
and they will be his people,
and God himself will be with
them as their God."
(Revelation 21:3)

Chapter 2

The Covenant Pattern:
God's Family and Mission

The story of the Bible moves forward from Eden with a profound question: How will God restore the world after humanity's fall into rebellion and exile? The answer appears again and again in a familiar pattern: God calls a people into covenant, forms them into a family, and gives them a mission to represent him. In other words, covenant is not an afterthought to grace – it is the very way grace works its way into history. From Noah to Abraham, from Israel to David, and finally through Jesus, God's mission unfolds in this pattern.

The biblical covenants provide the backbone of the restoration story.[19] Each covenant – with Noah, Abraham, Israel at Sinai, King David, and the New Covenant – reveals a rhythm of divine initiative, human calling, and eschatological hope.[20] God's goal was never just individual salvation. His aim has always been to restore a people – his family – through whom he would bless the nations (Gen. 12:3).

Scott Hahn explains that biblical covenants are primarily about relationship and family bond – divine kinship – not just formal agreements. In the ancient world, covenants often

---

19   A valuable resource is Paul R. Williamson, *Sealed with an Oath: Covenant in God's Unfolding Purpose* (Downers Grove, IL: IVP Academic, 2007). Williamson gives a readable overview of how each covenant shapes the Bible's story.

20   "Eschatological" refers to the end of the age or the fulfillment of God's purposes in history.

had the purpose of adopting or incorporating someone into a royal household.[21] In the Bible, God uses covenants to create a family that will reflect his rule in both heaven and on earth. Through the covenant, humanity is brought back into God's household with the mission of carrying his name before the world (cf. Exod. 19:5-6; Deut. 7:6; 1 Pet. 2:9).

The covenant at Mount Sinai marks a defining moment in God's plan: "At Sinai the Israelites learn who they are by learning whose they are – the name-bearers of Yahweh, Creator of heaven and earth."[22] Carmen Joy Imes describes the high priest as a visual model of what the whole covenant community is called to be: representing God's character and presence. She compares bearing God's name to having an invisible tattoo, permanent but visible to the nations through conduct and character.[23] In this way, restoration is never just about reconnecting with God vertically. It is also about living faithfully toward others horizontally.

Exile and a Broken Creation

The restoration story starts with honest realism about what was lost. Genesis 3-11 tells how sin shattered the world God made. Humanity's rebellion in Eden brought sin and death, and with them exile from God's presence. This

---

21 Scott W. Hahn, *Kinship by Covenant: A Canonical Approach to the Fulfillment of God's Saving Promises* (New Haven, CT: Yale University Press, 2009), 42. In his book, Hahn provides a widely cited treatment of covenant as the primary means of adoption and kinship in the ancient Near East and in the Bible.

22 Josh Philpot, "What 'Taking the Lord's Name in Vain' Really Means – Review: 'Bearing God's Name: Why Sinai Still Matters' by Carmen Joy Imes," on *The Gospel Coalition US Edition*, https://www.thegospelcoalition.org/reviews/bearing-god-name-sinai-carmen-joy-imes/, accessed on July 12, 2025.

23 Carmen Joy Imes, *Bearing God's Name: Why Sinai Still Matters* (Downers Grove, IL: IVP Academic, 2019), 48-52.

broke the relationship between God and humanity, marred the image of God in people, and let chaos loose in the world. The curse on the ground (Gen. 3:17-19) and Cain's murder of Abel (Gen. 4) show that sin affects families, land, and society alike. Yet even in judgment, God gives hope, as we saw in the *protoevangelium* ("first gospel") in Genesis 3:15.

Genesis 6 describes the second great rebellion. The "sons of God" (*bene ha'elohim*) are described as spiritual beings who have sexual union with human women and create offspring called *nephilim*.[24] These hybrid beings, the *nephilim*, unleash violence upon the earth. Second Temple writings like 1 Enoch saw this as a rebellion of divine beings against YHWH, adding to the corruption of creation and triggering the flood.[25]

The third rebellion, which resulted in the building of the Tower of Babel (Gen. 11:1-9), reveals humanity's drive for self-rule and fame. God responds by scattering and disinheriting the nations, confusing their languages. Yet, even here, the scattering is not the end of the story. In restorationist theology, exile is not only a punishment. It can also be preparation. God uses it to refine humanity's identity and character, teach dependence on him, and set the stage for hope.

---

24 The expression *bene ha'elohim* ("sons of God") in the Old Testament refers to heavenly beings who are part of God's divine council (cf. Job 1:6; 2:1; Ps. 89:6). In Genesis 6 we read how some of these beings left their proper place and had relations with human women, which resulted in the birth of the *nephilim*. Some translations render this as "race of giants," following later interpretations such as the Septuagint (LXX), which translates *nephilim* as *gigantes* ("giants"). The term, however, does not necessarily point to physical size; it can also refer to powerful or extraordinary beings. See Michael S. Heiser, *The Unseen Realm*, 102–111.

25 See 1 Enoch 6-36 and Jubilees 5:1-6 for early Jewish elaborations on the Genesis 6 story. Please note that both these books are non-canonical, but very influential in Second Temple Judaism.

Abraham and the Reversal of Babel

After these three rebellions, the Bible's restoration story takes a new turn with the call of Abraham (Gen. 12:1-3). His call is God's direct answer to the scattering of Babel. God tells Abraham, who was still called Abram at that time, to leave his homeland in the east, promising to make him into a great nation and to bless all "the families of the earth" through him. This covenant isn't just about Abram's personal destiny. It's about God's plan to bring the disinherited nations back into the family of God and back into his inheritance.

Michael Heiser connects this to the "Deuteronomy 32 worldview": after Babel, God assigned the nations to the rule of lesser spiritual beings,[26] while keeping Israel as his special inheritance (Deut. 32:8-9).[27] God's plan to reclaim those nations begins right here, with Abraham's family called to be a kingdom of priests (Exod. 19:6). Abraham becomes the father not only of Israel but of many nations. Through him, God begins to restore a broken world.

The Abrahamic covenant is not only spiritual but also profoundly concrete. God promises descendants, land, and his very own

---

26 The ESV translation of Deut. 32:8 says: "When the Most High gave to the nations their inheritance, when he divided mankind, he fixed the borders of the peoples according to the number of the sons of God." The ESV follows the Septuagint (LXX) tradition, as well as manuscripts found among the Dead Sea Scrolls (DSS). Some other English translations, such as the NIV, follow the - much newer - Masoretic tradition: "When the Most High gave the nations their inheritance, when he divided all mankind, he set up boundaries for the peoples according to the number of the sons of Israel." The LXX tradition seems to make more sense, because in the time of the rebellion of Babel, there was no Israel yet, so "sons of Israel" would have been an anachronism. Also, the Bible in other places never makes mention that the nations would be assigned to the authority and stewardship of the sons of Israel. So, we must opt for the LXX/DSS tradition, that the nations were assigned to the care of the "sons of God", *bene ha'elohim*, who were lower spiritual beings created by God.

27 Heiser, *The Unseen Realm*, 112-115. This "Deuteronomy 32 worldview" underlies much of Heiser's work and is a helpful way to frame the cosmic conflict in biblical theology. See also Daniel I. Block, *The Gods of the Nations: Studies in Ancient Near Eastern National Theology* (Grand Rapids, MI: Baker Academic, 2001), 21-25.

presence (Gen. 15; Gen. 17). Through it, God's plan is set in motion to renew creation through a covenant people. In restorationist theology, God's covenant with Abraham is a hinge: from Eden to the New Jerusalem, from scattering to gathering, from alienation to reconciliation. God's mission unfolds through a people that is called to reflect his character and to extend his blessing to all nations.

Israel as the Covenant People

Centuries later, God redeems Abraham's descendants from Egypt and forms them into a nation at Sinai. There, he gives them the *Torah,* not as a law that shows how they can earn salvation but as a guide that teaches them to live as a people who have been called for a greater purpose. Exodus 19:5-6 frames their calling in explicitly priestly and missional terms: "You shall be my treasured possession among all peoples… and you shall be to me a kingdom of priests and a holy nation." Carmen Joy Imes explains: "The Israelites had already been rescued from Egypt when they were given the law. God did not say to them, 'Do all these things and I will save you from slavery.' He saved them first and then gave them the gift that goes with salvation, instructions on how to live as free men and women."[28] YHWH gave the law as a fence for Israel, keeping out destructive influences and allowing life to flourish in their land.

The covenant at Sinai is a renewed commission very similar to the one God gave to Adam and Eve in Eden: to fill the earth, represent God's presence, and live as a light to the Gentiles (cf. Isa. 42:6). The land of Canaan was to become a new sacred space, a microcosm of restored creation where justice, worship, and covenant faithfulness were to dwell. But like the first humans, Israel failed. They fell into idolatry and injustice, leading to exile from the land: a replay of Eden's exile. This showed that

---

28   Imes, *Bearing God's Name*, 35.

the problem wasn't just oppression coming from the outside. The main problem was in the human heart. As Jeremiah 17:9 (NLT) says, "The human heart is the most deceitful of all things, and desperately wicked."

Even in failure, the prophets spoke of hope: one day, a New Covenant would be established. God would transform human hearts and inscribe his *Torah* within (Jer. 31:31-34; Ezek. 36:24-27). This New Covenant was inaugurated when the Holy Spirit was poured out in Jerusalem upon the disciples (Acts 2) and will be consummated when Jesus returns and "all Israel will be saved" (Rom. 11:26).

Yes, the Bible is profoundly Israel-centric. But the nations are always in view when you look at the biblical storyline of redemption and restoration: it is always about Israel and the nations. As Heiser notes, "It was God's intention, right on the heels of his decision to punish the nations, that the Israelites would serve as a conduit for their return to the true God."[29] God intended Israel to be the channel for bringing the nations back to himself, reversing their disinheritance at Babel. The restoration of Israel is therefore not the end point but the means to the restoration of God's reign over the whole earth (Zech. 14:9).

Pastoral Reflection: Living the Covenant Story Today

The covenant pattern of the Bible is not just an academic theme; it is the heartbeat of the Church's identity and mission. From Eden to Sinai, from Zion to the New Jerusalem, God is forming a people who bear his name, reflect his character, and extend his blessing.

For pastors and leaders, this means we are not just managing programs. Instead, we are tending a covenant family. In an age

---

29   Heiser, *The Unseen Realm*, 115.

of division, the Church is called to be a prophetic signpost to the one new man in Messiah – Jew and Gentile together. Therefore, it must recover its priestly calling. We are not only saved from sin and death but saved for the mission of God: to join his work of renewing creation through a faithful people.

This means that we build communities where justice, holiness, reconciliation, and Spirit-filled mission are not optional add-ons but central to who we are. And we must keep in view that the Bible tells a story of restoration, not replacement. God has not set aside his purposes for Israel, and the nations will be restored only in connection with her.

Restorationist theology calls us to preach and pastor with a vision that is both ancient and future – ancient, anchored in God's eternal promises; and future, fixed on the return of the King who will consummate the New Covenant. Until that day, we are called to live in covenant faithfulness, not as lifeless rule-keeping but as a vibrant, Spirit-filled witness to God's reign breaking into the world through the *ekklesia*.

"And I will make of you a great nation,
and I will bless you and make your name great,
so that you will be a blessing.
I will bless those who bless you,
and him who dishonors you I will curse,
and in you all the families of the earth
shall be blessed."
(Genesis 12:2-3)

Chapter 3

Israel, God's Restorative Instrument

The story of restoration advances as the covenant promises given to Abraham begin to take shape in the formation of a people – Israel – through whom God intends to bless the nations. This chapter traces how the Exodus, the covenant at Sinai, the Tabernacle, and the Promised Land together shape Israel into a priestly nation, entrusted to serve as God's restorative instrument in the world.

The Exodus: God Redeems a People for Himself

The Exodus is about so much more than the liberation of an oppressed people. It stands as the foundational act of divine redemption in the Hebrew Bible. God does not simply free Israel from slavery but redeems them for a covenant relationship. As declared in Exodus 6:6-7, God delivers them "with an outstretched arm," so that all may know YHWH is God. This echoes the act of creation – God brings order out of chaos – and points forward to the ultimate redemption in Messiah.

YHWH's victory over Pharaoh is also a defeat of Egypt's gods (Exod. 12:12). The Exodus reveals a cosmic spiritual struggle. Throughout the Bible, major events often reflect deeper spiritual realities (Deut. 32:8-9; Dan. 10:13,20). Michael Heiser explains that each of the plagues targeted specific Egyptian deities, demonstrating that YHWH alone holds ultimate power.[30] By rescuing Israel,

---

30   Heiser, *The Unseen Realm*, 150-151. John D. Currid, *Against the Gods: The*

God begins to restore the authority that was lost in Eden and re-establishes his rule through his people.

This event sets the pattern for how God will save in the future. In the original Greek of Luke 9:31, Jesus' transfiguration is called an *exodos*, linking his death and resurrection to a greater rescue. Where the first Exodus freed Israel from Egypt, Jesus' "exodus" frees all people from sin and death.

Sinai: The Formation of a Priestly Nation

The events leading up to Israel's arrival at Sinai – also called Horeb – are set within the larger pattern of the biblical feasts. The Feast of Passover (*Pesach*) and the Feast of Unleavened Bread (*Chag HaMatzot*) occur just before Israel departs from Egypt (Exod. 12-13). These feasts are not only commemorations of Israel's deliverance but prophetic markers that shape the nation's identity. The New Testament situates Jesus' crucifixion during Passover, further connecting his sacrifice to Israel's redemption story (Luke 22:15-20; 1 Cor. 5:7). The biblical author is making clear that Jesus provides a much greater redemption than Israel's exodus from Egypt.[31]

According to Jewish tradition, the giving of *Torah* at Mount Sinai took place on *Shavuot* (Feast of Weeks or Pentecost), fifty days after the Exodus.[32] There is a direct connection to the events in Acts 2, which also happened during Pentecost. There, the Spirit is poured

---

Polemical Theology of the Old Testament (Wheaton, Il: Crossway, 2013), explains that the battle between YHWH and the gods of Egypt is polemical theology, which is "monotheistic to the very core. The primary purpose of polemical theology is to demonstrate emphatically and graphically the distinction between the worldview of the Hebrews and the beliefs and practices of the rest of the ancient Near East."

31   G.K. Beale, *A New Testament Biblical Theology*, 484-485, for the typological connection between Passover, exodus, and Jesus' death.

32   The Hebrew word *Shavuot* can be translated as Pentecost. Pentecost is derived from the Greek word *pentekoste*, which means "fiftieth."

out, and God's *Torah* is written on human hearts (cf. Jer. 31:33; 2 Cor. 3:3), inaugurating the New Covenant. The storyline that began at Sinai finds initial fulfillment in the outpouring of the Holy Spirit on Jesus' first followers and looks forward to a time when all Israel will experience this promise at Messiah's return. The promise is not just for the firstfruits of Israel – Jesus' disciples – but for all Israel.

At Sinai, a people redeemed from slavery are called to be God's covenant partners, his "treasured possession… a kingdom of priests and a holy nation" (Exod. 19:5-6). This priestly identity is central to Israel's election, calling, and mission.[33] Carmen Joy Imes notes that the commandment in Exodus 20:7, that says "do not take the LORD's name in vain," is better translated as "do not bear the LORD's name in vain." This commandment is not merely a prohibition against profanity but an exhortation to faithfully represent God's name among the nations. This reframes *Torah* as a covenantal gift rather than a burden, a way of shaping a society of justice, worship, and prophetic witness (Deut. 4:5-8).[34]

The priestly identity of Israel mirrors the original calling of Adam and Eve: as humanity was commissioned to image God in the garden (Gen. 2:15), so Israel is commissioned to reflect God's

---

33   Biblical language about election and predestination primarily concerns the corporate calling of Israel as God's covenant people. While later Christian traditions developed doctrines of individual election to salvation or damnation, the original context of the biblical text highlights God's choice of Israel for a redemptive mission among the nations (cf. Deut. 7:6-8; Isa. 41:8-9; Rom. 9:4-5). When you take the ongoing calling of Israel out of the equation, you have to reapply texts that very clearly deal with Israel to something else.

34   See, for instance Carmen Joy Imes, *Bearing Yhwh's Name at Sinai*, 2-3. See also Imes, *Bearing God's Name*. Imes notes that the Hebrew word for "take", *nasa*, is better translated as "bear." The translation of the command then becomes: "you shall not bear the name of the LORD your God in vain." So, Israel is called to represent God well to all the other nations. They are called to represent God's character among the nations. Not taking or bearing the name of the LORD in vain is a command to live in a way that honors God's reputation, much like an ambassador carries the authority of the one who sends him.

character to the world.[35] The giving of the law at Sinai shapes a communal identity, and points forward to a day when, as Jeremiah says, God's *Torah* will be written upon human hearts (Jer. 31:31-34).

The Tabernacle: Eden Restored in Israel's Midst

The Feast of Tabernacles (*Sukkot*) also plays a significant role in this story of restoration. Leviticus 23:39-43 establishes the feast as a way for Israel to remember their time in the wilderness and how God provided for them. The people are commanded to live in booths to remember that they once lived in tents in the wilderness, and that God himself tabernacled among them. During *Sukkot*, they are commanded to celebrate God's faithful presence and anticipate the eschatological[36] hope of God dwelling with his people forever (cf. Zech. 14:16-19; Rev. 21:3). The God who was with them will be with them again.

God's covenant with Israel is not only about the *Torah* but even more about his presence. "Let them make me a sanctuary, that I may dwell in their midst" (Exod. 25:8). The tabernacle is the visible sign that God intends to dwell with Israel as a priestly nation on behalf of all of humanity, just as he walked with Adam and Eve in Eden.

The tabernacle was full of reminders of the Garden of Eden.[37] The lampstand (*menorah*) looked like a tree, pointing back to the

---

35   Gordon J. Wenham, "Sanctuary Symbolism in the Garden of Eden Story," in *Proceedings of the Ninth World Congress of Jewish Studies* (Jerusalem: World Union of Jewish Studies, 1986), 19-26, for the priestly connection between Eden and Israel.

36   "Eschatological" refers to the end of the age or the fulfillment of God's purposes in history. The prophets could see a future where God would dwell permanently with his people (cf. Ezek. 37:27; Rev. 21:3).

37   T. Desmond Alexander, *From Eden to the New Jerusalem: An Introduction to Biblical Theology* (Grand Rapids, MI: Kregel, 2008), 21-24, gives a concise overview of how the tabernacle and temple imagery point to a restored Eden.

tree of life (Exod. 25:31-40; cf. Gen. 2:9). Angels (*cherubim*) were woven into the curtain, just like the angels who guarded Eden after the exile (Exod. 26:31, cf. Gen. 3:24). This shows that while God's presence is holy, he made a way for people to be close to him again through covenant and atonement.

The tabernacle embodied the reality of Eden in miniature. It serves as a liturgical journey back to Eden's sacred mountain, where humanity was allowed to ascend to and dwell with God. The high priest was a new "Adam" who could come into God's presence to represent the people. Morales asserts that "the later high priest of Israel serving in the tabernacle must be understood fundamentally as an Adam-figure serving on the (architectural) mountain of God. ... The verbs used to describe Adam's work in [Genesis] 2:15, most accurately rendered 'to worship and obey,' are used together elsewhere in the Pentateuch only of the Levites in their tabernacle service (Num. 3:7-8; 8:26; 18:5-6). Adam is hereby depicted as the original high priest abiding in Eden, the original holy of holies."[38] He then explains that the association between Adam and the priest is strengthened by the parallel of Adam's post-transgression clothing and the clothing of the Levitical priests, who both needed their nakedness covered (Gen. 3:21; Exod. 20:26; 28:42), and the utilization of the same verb "to clothe" (*lābaš* in hiphil) and the same noun for "tunics" (*kuttōnet*).[39]

Beale adds the following connection between the tabernacle and the garden of Eden. He notes an increasing threefold gradation in holiness from outside the garden, proceeding inward. First, there is the area that surrounds the garden, which God calls "very

---

38   T. Desmond Alexander, *From Eden to the New Jerusalem*, 22-23.

39   L. Michael Morales, *Who Shall Ascend the Mountain of the Lord?* (Downers Grove, IL: IVP Academic, 2015), 53. Morales makes the connection between Adam and the priests by looking at the Hebrew words for "to clothe" and "tunics" in Gen. 3:21 and Lev. 8:13.

good" (Gen. 1:31), because it is God's creation. This relates to the outer court of the tabernacle. Then there is the garden, which is a sacred space separate from the ordinary world. This relates to the tabernacle's holy place, where God's priestly servant worships God by obeying him, by cultivating and guarding the garden. Eden itself is where God dwells. This relates to the tabernacle's Holy of Holies and is the source of both physical and spiritual life, symbolized by the rivers.[40]

The sacred space of the tabernacle made it possible for a holy God to have fellowship with people again – a people he had redeemed. However, God's continued presence with Israel depended on the two-way nature of the Sinai covenant. Israel had to live in covenant obedience to maintain their relationship with God and to be allowed to remain in the land of Canaan, their promised home. Ultimately, the tabernacle also points ahead to Jesus' incarnation[41] and to the outpouring of the Spirit at Pentecost in Acts 2, when God would come to live in his people through the Spirit.

The Land as Restorative Space

God's promise to Abraham included land (Gen. 15:18). This was partially fulfilled when Israel conquered Canaan and settled in the land. But the land was more than just territory – it was sacred space. Entering Canaan was like returning to Eden, a place where only YHWH was to be worshipped and where justice should prevail.

Deuteronomy 6 describes life in the land as a covenant blessing dependent on Israel's faithfulness. Laws about Sabbath and the year

---

40 G.K. Beale, *A New Testament Biblical Theology*, 608, 620-621.

41 The incarnation refers to the act by which the eternal Son of God took on human nature in the person of Messiah Jesus. In the incarnation, the divine Word (*Logos*) became fully human without ceasing to be fully divine (John 1:14; Phil. 2:6-8). It is the decisive moment in salvation history when God dwelt among humanity to reveal his character and accomplish redemption.

of jubilee show that the land and its people were meant to reflect God's justice: debt forgiveness, rest, and restoration of inheritance. Israel's calling included social justice, economic fairness, and caring for creation.

However, Israel's continued presence in the land was conditional. Disobedience would eventually lead to exile (Deut. 28), echoing humanity's exile from Eden. Yet even then, God promised restoration: "then the LORD your God will restore your fortunes and have mercy on you, and he will gather you again from all the peoples where the LORD your God has scattered you." (Deut. 30:3)

Pastoral Reflection: Shepherding a Covenant People

For today's pastors and leaders, the formation of Israel offers a paradigm for shaping covenant communities. We need to remember that the Church is not a spiritual club but a priestly people (1 Pet. 2:9) called to bear God's name among the nations. We as leaders must teach God's instruction not as a choice between law and grace but as the way of life for a redeemed people. This means cultivating justice, generosity, and stewardship of our environment as practical signs of our faithfulness to the covenant we are included in.

Above all, we need to recover the truth that God's presence should be at the center of our identity, personally, in our families, and in our churches. As we wait for the consummation of the New Covenant when Messiah returns, we are called to live in this present evil age[42] as members of a restored creation and as prophetic signs pointing toward the coming Messianic Age. Like ancient Israel, we are a holy people, set apart for God's purposes. We are people who can experience heaven touching earth in our daily lives.

---

42   A phrase from Galatians 1:4, referring to the current world system marked by sin and rebellion. Restorationist theology often emphasizes the contrast between this age and the coming Messianic Age when Jesus returns.

"I will make a covenant of peace with them;
it will be an everlasting covenant.
I will establish them and increase their numbers,
and I will put my sanctuary among them forever.
My dwelling place will be with them;
I will be their God, and they will be my people."
(Ezekiel 37:26-27 NIV)

Chapter 4

The Kingdom, the King, and Zion
God's Government Restored

Believers often forget that they are part of a Kingdom. Yet, the announcement of the Kingdom is central to the biblical storyline. In Matthew 24:14, Jesus speaks about the gospel of the Kingdom: "And this gospel of the kingdom will be proclaimed throughout the whole world as a testimony to all nations, and then the end will come."

What is this gospel of the Kingdom? Is it the message of salvation made possible through Jesus' death and resurrection? Is it the message of God's love and grace available for every human being? In our time, the gospel is sometimes reduced to a message of boundless inclusivity – a theological shift that often leads to hyper-grace or even universalism[43] – as though the Kingdom could be proclaimed without the necessity of repentance, without the light of God's judgment, and without the call to a life of obedience. As essential as love and grace are, this is not how the Bible itself defines the gospel.

The English uses the term "gospel" when the Greek uses the term *euaggelion*. The Dutch word *evangelie* and the French word

---

Hyper-grace refers to recent movements that emphasize the radical nature of God's grace while minimizing – or sometimes even denying – the biblical necessity of repentance, sanctification, and perseverance. Universalism (often in the form of "ultimate reconciliation") teaches that all people will eventually be saved, regardless of their response to the gospel. Both approaches deviate from the biblical witness that the Kingdom comes through both judgment and restoration, and that salvation is received by believing in Messiah and living in loyalty to him.

évangile are derived from this Greek term, and so is the English verb "evangelize." A literal translation of *euaggalion* would be quite simple: good (*eu*) news (*aggelion*). So, the "gospel of the kingdom" would be "good news about the kingdom," and in this case, good news about God's Kingdom.

In the Roman Empire, the term *euaggelion* was also used widely. It would be used for the good news announcing that an emperor had conquered a territory and now had become the supreme ruler over it, or when a new emperor had ascended the throne in Rome. The Calendar Inscription of Priene, dating back to 9 BCE, is a great example, which says, "the birthday of the god Augustus was the beginning of the good tidings [*euaggelion*] for the world that came by reason of him."[44]

The Gospel of Matthew opens with this proclamation of John the Baptizer and Jesus: "Repent, for the kingdom of heaven is at hand" (Matt. 3:2; 4:17). This proclamation captures the essence of the biblical gospel, the biblical *euaggelion*. To confirm that point, we can look at the Old Testament and whether the ancient Greek translation of the Old Testament, the Septuagint (LXX), also uses the noun *euaggelion* or the related verb *euaggelizo*. Is there a linguistic continuity between the Greek of the Septuaguint and the Greek of the New Testament?

A key scripture in the LXX that uses the term *euaggelion* and clarifies its meaning from an Old Testament perspective is Isaiah

---

44 The full text of the calendar inscription of Priene reads: "It seemed good to the Greeks of Asia, in the opinion of the high priest Apollonius of Menophilus Azanitus: 'Since Providence, which has ordered all things and is deeply interested in our life, has set in most perfect order by giving us Augustus, whom she filled with virtue that he might benefit humankind, sending him as a savior, both for us and for our descendants, that he might end war and arrange all things, and since he, Caesar, by his appearance (excelled even our anticipations), surpassing all previous benefactors, and not even leaving to posterity any hope of surpassing what he has done, and since the birthday of the god Augustus was the beginning of the good tidings [εὐαγγέλιον] for the world that came by reason of him,' which Asia resolved in Smyrna."

52:7: "How beautiful upon the mountains are the feet of him who brings good news (LXX: *euaggelizomenou*), who publishes peace... who says to Zion, 'Your God reigns.'" The gospel, then, is first and foremost a royal announcement: Israel's God is taking his throne through his anointed King. The "good news," then, is not merely about individual salvation but about the restoration of God's reign through Messiah Jesus.

For Paul, this "salvation" in its ultimate form is future (Rom. 5:9-10; 10:9,13; 13:11) and collective (Rom. 9:27; 10:1; 11:26) but individuals already participate in this salvation through embracing the gospel.[45] Zechariah 14:9 declares that the LORD, YHWH, will be King over all the earth. This eschatological vision fuels the proclamation of the gospel in the New Testament. When John the Baptizer and Jesus in Matthew proclaim, "Repent, for the kingdom of heaven is at hand," this underscores the expectation that God's heavenly rule would soon break into the present evil age (Gal. 1:4). So, from both the Old Testament and New Testament perspective, the gospel is not the message of Jesus' death and resurrection but rather the proclamation that Israel's long-expected King and Kingdom would arrive soon. For this to happen, Jesus would have to die on the cross, rise from the dead, ascend to heaven, and return to earth.

The Son of David and the Zion Pattern

The covenant with David (2 Sam. 7) marks a decisive moment in the biblical storyline. God promises David an everlasting dynasty. His son is to build a house for God's name. This royal covenant builds on earlier covenants (with Abraham and with

---

45   See Craig Keener, "Gospel, Good News," on *St Andrews Encyclopaedia of Theology* (https://www.saet.ac.uk/Christianity/GospelGoodNews), accessed on July 9, 2025.

Israel at Mount Sinai) and connects kingship with the temple, Mount Zion, and God's own presence.

David's establishment of Jerusalem as the political and spiritual capital of Israel is not accidental. Jerusalem is linked to Eden on multiple levels. The first one is that Mount Zion, the site of the temple, is where Eden was also located, the cosmic mountain where heaven and earth meet. Second: the temple reflects imagery from the Garden of Eden, with garden motifs, cherubim, and a tree-like menorah.

The third one is that David purchases the threshing floor of Araunah the Jebusite on Mount Moriah to be the site of the altar (2 Sam. 24:18-25). This is the same hill where Abraham almost sacrificed Isaac (Gen. 22), and where Solomon later builds the temple (2 Chron. 3:1). Thus, Mount Moriah, Mount Zion, and the Temple Mount are traditionally understood as the same location and, in some Jewish traditions, identified with Eden itself. David insists on paying for Araunah's threshing floor, refusing to offer YHWH "that which costs me nothing" (2 Sam. 24:24). This recalls Abraham's willingness to offer Isaac but then, right before he planned to kill Isaac, God supernaturally provides a substitute, a ram. Just as God provided a ram in Abraham's day, David prepares the very place where ultimate atonement would one day be made by Jesus, David's greater Son.

Remarkably, Araunah is a Jebusite, one of the original inhabitants of the land. The fact that he was included in the story regarding the temple hints at the future inclusion of the nations. The worship center of Israel is established with the cooperation of a Gentile. This scene foreshadows the "one new man" unity described in Ephesians 2:15.

The Rebellion of the Nations and Psalm 2

Psalm 2 is foundational for understanding biblical kingship and global mission. It opens with the nations raging and the peoples plotting against YHWH and his Anointed (Hebrew: *Mashiach*, in English: Messiah or Christ from the Greek *Christos*). This rebellion against God's authority is not limited to the ancient world. It echoes in the present-day rejection by the masses of God, his Messiah, his Word, his covenant people, and even Mount Zion itself, where Messiah will one day reign. Psalm 2 frames human history as a conflict between human rulers and God himself.

God does not respond with fear but with laughter. He installs his King on Zion and declares, "You are my Son; today I have begotten you" (Ps. 2:7). This verse is quoted in Acts 13:33 and Hebrews 1:5 in reference to Jesus, showing its messianic fulfillment in him. The Psalm ends with an urgent invitation: "Kiss the Son, lest he be angry, and you perish in the way, for his wrath is quickly kindled. Blessed are all who take refuge in him."

Psalm 2 underscores the ongoing importance of Zion, the kingship of Jesus, and the nations' resistance to God's purposes. We see the rebellion it describes play out in today's world. Yet, this Psalm also affirms that Messiah will inherit the nations and not just Israel: "Ask of me, and I will make the nations your heritage, and the ends of the earth your possession" (Ps. 2:8). This promise, first given to Abraham's offspring (Gen. 22:18), has begun to be fulfilled as Jesus commissions the Church to reach the nations (Matt. 28:18-20). But its complete fulfillment will come when Jesus returns and all nations come under his rule.

The Already and Not Yet of the Kingdom

Restorationist theology emphasizes that the Kingdom was inaugurated at Jesus' first coming but awaits consummation at his return. Jesus' resurrection and exaltation mark the beginning of his rule (Acts 2:32-36). Still, the world is not yet fully subject to him (Heb. 2:8). The present age remains under the influence of darkness (Gal. 1:4), yet signs of the age to come break in through healing, deliverance, and Spirit-empowered witness.

There are different schools of thought within Restorationism regarding the "already/not yet" dynamic. Some are cautious – wary of sounding too much like realized eschatology, which, in their minds, focuses too much on the here and now, while de-emphasizing a yet future fulfilment of prophetic texts, resisting triumphalist claims that all Kingdom benefits are fully available now. Others acknowledge that signs of the Kingdom, such as healing and deliverance, are signs that point forward to the coming Messianic Age (Rom. 8:23).[46]

While we cannot presumptuously claim all the blessings of the coming Kingdom, we should trust that the Spirit continues to break into our age, offering glimpses of what is to come. These signs are like the down payment (*arrabōn*) Paul mentions in Ephesians 1:14, giving us a foretaste of a redeemed creation. They are meant to stir our longing for the fullness ahead and invite those who have not yet responded to the gospel of the Kingdom.

The Church as the Renewed Qahal

The New Testament Church is not a new invention but the renewal and extension of the Old Testament *qahal*, the assembly of God's

---

46   For a scholarly treatment of the "already/not yet" dynamic of the Kingdom, see George Eldon Ladd, *The Presence of the Future: The Eschatology of Biblical Realism* (Grand Rapids: Eerdmans, 1974). He writes: "the Kingdom of God is the redemptive reign of God dynamically active to establish his rule among men, and that this Kingdom, which will appear as an apocalyptic act at the end of the age, has already come into human history in the person and mission of Jesus to overcome evil, to deliver men from its power, and to bring them into the blessings of God's reign. [Therefore] the Kingdom of God involves two great moments: fulfillment within history, and consummation at the end of history." (p.218).

covenant people. Stephen in Acts 7:38 refers to Israel at Sinai as the "church" (*ekklesia*) in the wilderness. The term *ekklesia* in the Septuagint translates *qahal* dozens of times. It thereby reveals the continuity between Israel and the early Jesus-movement.[47]

This renewed *qahal* is founded on Jesus Messiah, the true King from David's line. Through his death and resurrection, the community was opened to both Jews and Gentiles, united as one Body (Eph. 2:11-22). Yet this unity does not erase their ethnic distinctions. Paul presents a future hope: all Israel will be saved (Rom. 11:26), and the nations will join Israel in worshipping in Jerusalem (Zech. 14:16). So, the restored people of God are already being gathered but they are not yet complete. We still await the full regathering of Israel and the healing of the nations under Jesus' kingship from Mount Zion.

Pastoral Reflection: Proclaiming the Kingdom Today

Pastors and leaders must fully grasp the gospel as the royal announcement of the coming King and his Kingdom. Too often, we reduce the gospel to a message about individual forgiveness, salvation, and eternal life. But the biblical gospel proclaims the kingship of Jesus, the restoration of Israel, and the inclusion of the Gentile nations in God's restored global family.

When we stay true to the gospel of the Kingdom, our goal is no longer to make converts but to make disciples. We call people not just to believe in Jesus but to submit to him as King. We will teach them a Kingdom worldview. In that worldview justice, holiness, and mission flow from allegiance to Messiah. Moreover, we will prepare our congregations to live in the tension of the already and not yet.

---

47 Skip Moen has an extensive discussion on the Hebrew words *qahal* and *ĕdah*, and the Greek words *ekklesia* and *sunagoge* on his website. Skip Moen, "The Church," on https://skipmoen.com/2009/05/the-church/, accessed on July 10, 2025.

We trust God for signs of the Kingdom in the current age while we wait in eager anticipation for the Kingdom's consummation. The King is coming! The Kingdom will be established!

We live in the days of Psalm 2. The nations rage against YHWH, his *Mashiach*, and Zion but Messiah is already enthroned in heaven, prepared for the moment of the full establishment of the Kingdom here on earth.[48] Therefore, we must disciple our people to live in that reality: to bear witness to his coming reign, and to give the world a foretaste of the world to come.

---

48 A helpful article exploring these aspects of Psalm 2 is: Jeff Kennedy, "Is Jesus the Messianic Davidide of Psalm 2?", on https://www.christotelic.faith/articles/is-jesus-the-messianic-davidide-of-psalm-2, accessed on July 10, 2025.

"He who sits in the heavens laughs;
the LORD holds them in derision.
Then he will speak to them in his wrath,
and terrify them in his fury, saying,
"As for me, I have set my King
on Zion, my holy hill."
(Psalm 2:4-6)

Chapter 5

The Prophets and the Hope of Restoration: Proclaiming the New Covenant in Exile and Return

The prophetic literature of the Hebrew Bible emerged from within the framework of the covenants, not as disconnected writings. The prophets were not independent religious visionaries but covenant prosecutors, intercessors, and heralds of restoration. Their task was to call Israel back to faithfulness to their covenant with YHWH, to expose injustice and idolatry, and to announce the redemptive acts God would perform in the future.

Throughout the prophetic books, the *Nevi'im*, we see a constant tension between judgment and hope. The prophets confront Israel over covenant violations, frequently referencing the curses described in Deuteronomy 28-29. Yet they also look ahead to a time of restoration, grounded in God's promises to Abraham, Moses, and David. This prophetic hope is expressed most clearly during and after the Babylonian exile, when Israel's identity and purpose were deeply challenged.

The failure of Israel's monarchy and priesthood is not the end of the story. It sets the stage for the renewal of both under the messianic figure anticipated by the Latter Prophets (Isaiah-Malachi). These prophets envisioned a time when the scattered exiles would return to their land, a new David would rule, the temple would be rebuilt, and the Spirit would be poured out on all flesh.

The visions that these prophets had are ultimately forward-looking. Though based in covenant history, they go beyond present troubles and point to God's future renewal of Israel and the nations. Restoration isn't simply returning to what was lost. It is God's powerful work of making all things new. For the prophets, hope was always on the horizon.

The New Testament apostles follow the pattern of the prophets, announcing that many of God's promises to Israel are being fulfilled through Jesus. Yet this fulfillment is only the beginning. Much remains to be accomplished when he returns. The gospel does not depart from the message of the prophets. It marks the start of their fulfillment. Through Jesus' first coming, God's Kingdom has been inaugurated on earth, though its consummation is still to come.

Exile: Covenant Curse and the Shattering of Identity

The exile of both the northern kingdom (Israel in 722 BCE) and the southern kingdom (Judah in 586 BCE) marks the collapse of Israel's covenant identity. This was not a random historical event, but the result of the covenant curses described in Deuteronomy 28-29. Israel's disobedience, seen in its idolatry, injustice, and rejection of YHWH's prophets, lead to the loss of land, temple, and sovereignty.

The land, which had once been sacred space for covenant life, is now desolate. The temple, which had represented God's dwelling among his people, is destroyed. The Davidic monarchy, which was to be eternal (2 Sam. 7:16), lies in ruins. The exile calls into question not only Israel's future but also whether God is truly faithful to his promises. Could anything rekindle their hope?

We must realize, though, that exile is not simply punishment. Exile is always disciplinary and leads to repentance, forgiveness, and ultimately restoration. Through exile, God purges idolatry and brings Israel to a place of humility and longing. Ezekiel 36-37 and Isaiah 40-66 present a people broken but not forsaken, a people who will be renewed by the Spirit and regathered into the land under the reign of Messiah.

Exile is therefore both judgment and preparation. It demonstrates the severity of covenant violation but also opens the door to a deeper restoration. In Second Temple Judaism, after the Babylonian exile, many Jews perceived that, despite a return to the land, exile had not fully ended and Israel still awaited a full restoration.[49] This unfulfilled hope provides the background for the coming of Jesus, who is seen as the One who inaugurates a return from exile in a deeper, spiritual sense.

From a restorationist perspective, the exile is much more than a backdrop to history. It is a theological event that still shapes God's redemptive mission. The return from exile is both literal (the regathering of Jews to their land) and spiritual (the transformation of hearts and identity through the New Covenant). The prophets' cries from exile become cries of hope, ultimately answered in Messiah.

The Prophetic Vision of Restoration

The prophetic literature of the Hebrew Bible is shaped by themes of divine judgment and eschatological hope. The prophets confront Israel's covenant unfaithfulness and announce exile as a consequence of disobedience, yet they also paint a powerful vision of restoration. This restoration is far more than a return from Babylon. It centers on Israel's renewal, the gathering of the nations, and the coming reign of YHWH through his Anointed.

---

49   N. T. Wright, *The New Testament and the People of God* (Minneapolis: Fortress Press, 1992), 268-269.

A Restoration Bigger than the Return from Babylon

Jeremiah, Isaiah, Ezekiel, and the Twelve[50] all envision a day when God will not only bring Israel back to the land but will also renew them from within.

This restoration is described in terms of renewal of the covenant, spiritual transformation, and the re-establishment of Zion as the epicenter of global worship. Jeremiah famously prophesies: "Behold, the days are coming, declares the LORD, when I will make a new covenant with the house of Israel and the house of Judah" (Jer. 31:31).

Isaiah envisions a future where Israel becomes the "light for the nations" (Isa. 49:6) God always intended it to be, and Mount Zion is lifted up as the place from which *Torah* and peace will go forth (Isa. 2:1-4). This hope is not merely nationalistic. It is cosmic and redemptive, aimed at reversing the curse of exile and restoring all creation under YHWH's rule as the divine King. It is a compelling promise of restoration.

Echoes from the Second Temple Period

Second Temple Jewish literature confirms that this prophetic hope shaped Jewish eschatological expectations during the time of Jesus. The Psalms of Solomon, written in the first century BCE, reflect an expectation of a Davidic messiah who would "gather a holy people, whom he will lead in righteousness" (Pss.Sol. 17:26).[51] The Dead Sea Scrolls also show that the Qumran community expected a messianic figure through whom God would restore Israel and renew the covenant community.[52]

---

50   The Twelve are the "Minor Prophets" of the Hebrew Bible.

51   The Psalms of Solomon were likely written in the late 1st century BCE, probably in a Pharisaic context, and survive in Greek manuscripts.

52   Some DSS scholars have held the position that this messianic figure is twofold: a

These writings confirm a belief that restoration is not simply about a return to the land or the reconstruction of the temple. Restoration involves purification, righteousness, and a renewed presence of God among his people.

The Role of the Spirit

Central to the prophetic vision is the outpouring of the Spirit. Isaiah 44:3 speaks of a day when God will "pour water on the thirsty land, and streams on the dry ground... I will pour my Spirit upon your offspring." Joel echoes this: "And it shall come to pass afterward, that I will pour out my Spirit on all flesh" (Joel 2:28).

This outpouring of the Spirit marks a deep inner renewal for God's people: hearts are transformed (Deut. 30:6), God's *Torah* is written within (Jer. 31:33), and their covenant identity is brought back to life. The Spirit is God's agent of restoration, leading Israel out of exile into renewed obedience and empowering them for global witness. Jews during the Second Temple period anticipated an end-time outpouring of God's Holy Spirit in correlation with the Messianic Age and a renewed Israel.[53] As a result of this end-time outpouring of the Holy Spirit, God's children would be able to glorify him and serve him in sincerity and truth.[54] This outpouring is closely tied to Israel's election. It is a promise given first to the Jewish people, restoring them to covenant faithfulness, and then

---

priestly messiah from Aaron and a royal messiah from Israel's line. However, this view has been challenged by other scholars, who just see one messianic figure. For an in-depth discussion, see Jona Lendering, "Qumran's Dual Messianism," *Livius. org* (2001), https://www.livius.org/articles/religion/messiah/messiah-9-two-messiahs/ (accessed on 22 Nov. 2025).

53   Ben Frostad, "Spirit in Judaism – part 1: Second Temple Era," *Segullah*, October 27 2017, https://www.segullah.net/spirit-judaism-part-1/ (accessed on 22 Nov. 2025).

54   Francis-David Athelstan Scalzo, *The Jewish Basis for the Born Again Experience in John 3* (A Dissertation Submitted to the Faculty of the John W. Rawlings School of Divinity in Lynchburg, VA, 2022), 212.

extended to the nations, who are grafted into that same promise through Messiah (see Rom. 11).

A Unified Expectation

The prophets closely connect Israel's national restoration with the renewal of the whole world. Israel's redemption serves as the driving force for global renewal. As Zephaniah prophesies: "At that time I will change the speech of the peoples to a pure speech, that all of them may call upon the name of the LORD and serve him with one accord" (Zeph. 3:9).

In other words, the prophetic vision goes beyond Israel's survival and restoration. It embraces the transformation of the nations and all of creation (Isa. 11:6-9; 65:17-25). The return from exile becomes a signpost, pointing to a greater reality: the renewed presence and reign of God among all peoples, just as in Eden.

Ezekiel 37 and the New Covenant

The vision of the valley of dry bones in Ezekiel 37 stands as a key prophetic passage for grasping both Israel's national and spiritual restoration. In this striking vision, God brings Ezekiel to a valley filled with dry bones. These "dry bones" represent "the whole house of Israel" (Ezek. 37:11). And then God commands him to prophesy. As Ezekiel speaks, the bones come together, are clothed with flesh, and finally receive *ruach* (Spirit, breath) – the very life of God.

This vision is not merely an allegory for spiritual renewal. In its original context, it speaks of the revival of Israel as a people, nationally and spiritually. Israel, exiled and fragmented, is brought back to life and reconstituted as one people under one King. As Ezekiel 37:14 declares: "I will put my Spirit within you, and you shall live, and I will place you in your own land."

The New Covenant and Israel's Corporate Resurrection

Restorationist theology understands Ezekiel 37 as a prophetic image of the New Covenant. It is a tangible promise to Israel, not a spiritual abstraction. The chapter culminates in the promise of a *berit shalom*, a "covenant of peace," which is also described as an everlasting covenant (Ezek. 37:26). This closely connects to Jeremiah 31:31-34, where God promises a New Covenant with the house of Israel and Judah.

Messianic Jewish scholar Daniel Juster affirms the link between the Kingdom of God and Israel: "The New Covenant promises the worldwide Kingdom of God in its connection to Israel. God makes His covenant with the nations through Israel."[55] In other words, the New Covenant is established first with Israel, and it is through Israel that blessing flows to the nations. The Church does not replace Israel but shares in Israel's covenant through faith in Messiah. Likewise, David Stern notes: "There remain promises to national Israel, the Jewish people, in which Gentile nations corporately and Gentile believers individually have no direct share."[56] The unity of Jew and Gentile in Messiah does not erase Israel's national destiny. Rather, it confirms it.

These passages, especially Ezekiel 37, highlight Israel's corporate resurrection – both physical and spiritual – as central to biblical hope for the future. In this sweeping vision of restoration, the regathering of the exiles and the outpouring of the Spirit are inseparably linked.

---

55   Daniel Juster & Keith (Asher) Intrater, *Israel, the Church, and the Last Days* (Shippensburg, PA: Destiny Image Publishers, 2003), 27.

56   David H. Stern, *Restoring the Jewishness of the Gospel* (Clarksville, MD: Messianic Jewish Publishers, 2010), 25.

The Shepherd-King and Messianic Hope

The second half of Ezekiel 37 shifts focus to Israel's reunification under one King: "My servant David shall be king over them, and they shall all have one shepherd" (Ezek. 37:24). This is not a nostalgic return to David himself but a messianic prophecy of the coming descendant of David who will unify Israel and Judah and shepherd them. Messianic expectation during the Second Temple period commonly interpreted this "David" as Messiah.

The Targum Jonathan interprets Ezekiel 37:25 with explicit reference to "My servant David as their prince for all time." In other words, a future ruler from the line of David will rule over "the land that I gave to My servant Jacob and in which your ancestors dwelt."[57] The New Testament clearly identifies Jesus as the Davidic Shepherd-King (cf. John 10:11; Rev.5:5). Jesus is the one through whom Israel will be fully restored, and through whom the Gentiles are included in the renewed covenant community.

Spirit-Empowered Revival and the Beginning of Fulfillment

The image of breath (*ruach*) entering the reassembled bodies in Ezekiel's vision of the dry bones unmistakably points to the Holy Spirit as the agent of renewal. In Acts, this promise begins to unfold in distinct stages: first in Jerusalem among Jews (Acts 2), then in Samaria among Samaritans (Acts 8), and finally among Gentiles (Acts 10-11).

As James T. Mace shows, the Samaritan Pentecost (Acts 8) stands apart from the Jewish and Gentile episodes. While something visible clearly occurs – Simon "sees" an extraordinary manifestation – Luke's theological focus centers on the apostles' laying on of hands. This act is a deliberate sign: the Samaritans,

---

57 *Targum Jonathan* on Ezekiel 37:25 on Sefaria, https://www.sefaria.org/Ezekiel.37.25, accessed on July 10, 2025.

long despised by Judeans, are now fully welcomed as descendants of the house of Israel, restored and reconciled with Judah under the New Covenant. Here, unity and acceptance take precedence over external manifestations. Thus, Acts 8 dramatizes the fulfillment of prophetic hope (Ezekiel 37), in which both houses of Israel are reunited as one people under Messiah.[58]

Acts 2 recounts the outpouring of the Spirit on Jewish disciples in Jerusalem during *Shavuot* (Pentecost), a festival deeply rooted in the Sinai covenant (cf. Exod. 19; Lev. 23). This event inaugurates the New Covenant, yet it is only the first stage. The complete national revival of Israel, envisioned by Ezekiel, remains unfulfilled and still lies ahead.

The Apostle Paul affirms this future moment: "For if their rejection means the reconciliation of the world, what will their acceptance mean but life from the dead?" (Rom. 11:15). Ezekiel's prophecy and Paul's vision meet here, both portraying Israel's restoration as a dramatic resurrection – "life from the dead."

The Restoration of Israel and the Inclusion of the Nations

The prophetic vision of restoration always reaches beyond ethnic Israel. While Ezekiel, Isaiah, and other prophets begin with Israel's revival and regathering, they also foresee the nations joining in God's redemptive plan. God's purpose has always been to create one people, both faithful Israelites and redeemed Gentiles together. This is the very heart of Paul's "one new man" teaching in Ephesians 2:14-16.

Ezekiel 37's vision unfolds in two movements: first, the resurrection of Israel in the valley of dry bones (vv.1-14); second,

---

58   James T. Mace, *Ensign for the Nations: The Heilsgeschichtlicher Phase of Messianic Reunification in Luke–Acts* (M.Litt. thesis, University of St. Andrews, 2012), 2, 30-35.

the reunification of the divided kingdoms under a single ruler (vv.15-28). These are not separate prophecies but together form a unified picture of national restoration and covenant renewal. Under a Messianic King, this reunited Kingdom of Israel will once again shine God's light to the nations, drawing them back into God's family: "My dwelling place shall be with them, and I will be their God, and they shall be my people. Then the nations will know that I am the LORD who sanctifies Israel, when my sanctuary is in their midst forevermore" (Eze. 37:27-28).

Paul's letters echo Ezekiel's imagery. In Ephesians 2:11-22, Paul describes how Gentiles, once "strangers to the covenants of promise," have now been "brought near by the blood of Christ." Through the cross, Jesus has broken down the dividing wall of hostility and created "in himself one new man in place of the two." This is the renewal of the *qahal* – God's covenant assembly – now expanded to include the redeemed from every nation.

In this unified Body, there is still room for distinction between Jew and Gentile, and between the various ethnic groups within the Body. Paul is clear about a future role for ethnic Israel (Rom. 11:25-29) but at the same time, he emphasizes that salvation comes to all through faith in Messiah. Ariel Blumenthal, in his book One New Man, asserts that the apostle Paul "taught a kind of unity [between Jew and Gentile] amidst continuing distinctions – not a bland uniformity; he saw that if God's 'gifts and calling' for Israel are 'irrevocable' (Rom. 11:29), then it means that the integrity of Jewish identity—in Christ—must somehow be preserved. ... Conversely, ... Paul was not in favor of somehow diluting Jewish uniqueness by Gentile Christians taking on some kind of quasi-Jewish identity."[59] Paul's "one new man" vision embraces Israel's unique identity while

59   Ariel Laurence Blumenthal, *One New Man: Reconciling Jew & Gentile in One Body of Christ* (Sisters, OR: Deep River Books, 2018), 77.

fully welcoming Gentiles, showing that genuine unity comes from a shared allegiance to Messiah rather than from cultural uniformity.

The Role of the Fivefold Ministry

Unity, however, does not arise spontaneously. Paul is clear in Ephesians 4:11-13 that Jesus gave apostles, prophets, evangelists, pastors, and teachers to the Body of Messiah "to equip the saints for the work of ministry, for building up the body of Christ." The fivefold ministry is not an optional structure but essential to the Church's growth into maturity and unity.

The fivefold gifts are not merely vocational titles but function as covenant leadership roles. They serve to call the Body of Messiah into its Kingdom identity, discipling both Jewish and Gentile believers to walk in their unique callings and shared inheritance. Juster's vision aligns with Restorationism's view that the Spirit-empowered, apostolic Church is grafted into Israel's mission, joining with faithful Israel in God's ongoing purpose to be a light to the nations.

The Role of Spiritual Gifts

The restoration of God's people also requires the activation of spiritual gifts. As Paul explains in 1 Corinthians 12:7, these gifts are distributed by the Spirit "for the common good." They are not tools for personal fulfillment but instruments of mutual edification, unity, and effective witness. When functioning properly, these gifts help the one new man to operate as a Spirit-filled priesthood (1 Pet. 2:9). Spiritual gifts, including prophecy, healing, and tongues, were present in the early Jewish Jesus movement and served to confirm the message to both the circumcised and the uncircumcised, as the gospel spread among Jews and Gentiles alike. This spiritual empowerment is not for individual status but for missional service and unity within the covenant community. These gifts help the *ekklesia* to live as a Kingdom people, expressing both power and humility in service to Israel and the nations.

As the fivefold ministry equips the saints and the gifts of the Spirit are mobilized, the one new man becomes a visible sign of God's Kingdom breaking into this world, a foretaste of the fullness that will come when Messiah returns to reign from Zion.

Jesus, the Incarnate Angel of YHWH

One of the most profound and mysterious themes running through the Hebrew Bible is the identity and activity of the Angel of YHWH. In numerous appearances, this figure both represents YHWH and is identified with YHWH himself. These appearances raise an important theological question: how can the Angel of YHWH be both distinct from and identical with YHWH?

Michael Heiser explains this tension as a deliberate revelation of a visible YHWH sent from the invisible YHWH. If humans encountered the invisible YHWH, their senses would not be able to process it. An encounter like this would even be deadly.[60] As God said to Moses, "You cannot see my face, for man shall not see me and live" (Exod. 33:20). So, the visible YHWH is YHWH in a form that the human senses can process.

The Angel of YHWH is so much more than a created angelic being. He speaks as God (cf. Gen. 22:15-18), receives worship (Judg. 13:20-22), forgives sins (Zech. 4), and even identifies himself with God's name (Exod. 3:2-6). He is a visible manifestation of the invisible God, YHWH, in a form humans can process. As Doug Van Dorn asserts, commenting on how early Church Fathers like Justin Martyr interpreted *Torah*, "If the Fathers are correct, then the author of Genesis knew a second Yahweh. He knew different Persons to be YHWH. Moses was a monotheist but not a Unitarian.

---

60   Heiser, *The Unseen Realm*, 124.

Neither were the Patriarchs. ... The Angel is the most important form of revelation in their days. They interact with the Angel on a daily basis."[61]

Theologically, what the Hebrew Bible teaches about the Angel of YHWH prepares the way for the incarnation. Jesus, the Word made flesh, is the visible image of the invisible God (Col. 1:15). Jesus is not merely an angel or even a high-ranking messenger or prophet. He is the Angel of YHWH, the second person of the Trinity in pre-incarnate form. In other words, the Angel of YHWH in the Old Testament is the same divine person who took on flesh in the New Testament. Jesus did not become the Son at his birth in Bethlehem. He has always existed as the sent One of the Father. He is the Word (*logos*), who was the agent in creation and the Angel who had lunch with Abraham, made flesh.[62]

Jewish texts from the Second Temple period, such as those written by Philo of Alexandria, and rabbinic sources before the second century, accepted the idea of two divine figures who shared the same divine essence. Michael Heiser writes, "There was no sense of a violation of monotheism since either figure was indeed Yahweh. There was no second distinct god running the affairs of the cosmos."[63] Jewish scholar Alan Segal asserts, "Philo could even use the phrase 'second God' to describe the *logos* without thinking that he had violated the monotheistic basis of his religion."[64] Only

---

61   Doug Van Dorn, *The Angel of the LORD: A Biblical, Historical, and Theological Study* (Erie, CO: Waters of Creation, 2020), 33. See also Alan F. Segal, *Two Powers in Heaven: Early Rabbinic Reports About Christianity and Gnosticism* (Leiden: Brill Academic Publishers, 2002), 183-185.

62   Heiser, *The Unseen Realm*, 129-130, referring to Genesis 1, Genesis 15:1-6) and John 1.

63   Michael Heiser, "Two Powers in Heaven," on https://drmsh.com/the-naked-bible/two-powers-in-heaven/, accessed on July 9, 2025.

64   Alan F. Segal, *Two Powers in Heaven*, 183.

later, in the second century CE, in reaction to early Christian claims about Jesus, was this doctrine declared heretical in Jewish circles.[65]

The "two powers in heaven" understanding does not lead to polytheism. Rather, it points toward the mystery of the Trinity, which is progressively revealed throughout Scripture. The Father sends the Son (who appeared as the Angel of YHWH), and both the Father and the Son send the Spirit. The Holy Spirit, too, is present throughout the Old Testament as the one who empowers creation (Gen. 1:2), fills prophets (Num. 11:25), and anoints kings (1 Sam. 16:13). The Spirit is not an impersonal force but a divine person who speaks, guides, and grieves (Isa. 63:10).

This Old Testament affirms the triune nature of God without resorting to later Greek philosophical approaches. Jesus is not an innovation. He is the incarnated self-revelation of the same God who walked in Eden, spoke at Sinai, and dwelled in the tabernacle.

The relevance of this theology for Restorationism is immense. It reveals that God has always desired to dwell among his people. The incarnation is not a change in God's plan but its climax. The same divine presence who led Israel through the wilderness is the one who now leads his renewed people through the Spirit, empowering them for mission until Messiah returns.

Pastoral Reflection: Preaching and Living Israel's Hope While Welcoming the Nations

The prophetic books of the Hebrew Bible call pastors and leaders to hold two truths together without confusion: 1) God will literally restore Israel – people, land, and kingdom – because of his irrevocable covenants, and 2) that same restoration overflows to

---

65   Michael Heiser, "Two Powers in Heaven."

76

bless the nations who are grafted into Israel's hope (Isa. 49:6; Rom. 11:17-24). Below are four pastoral commitments that will help us keep those truths in proper order.

1. Guard Israel's unique covenant promises.

"*Eretz Israel*" (the land of Israel), Jerusalem, and the Davidic throne remain Israel's God-given inheritance (Jer. 31:35-37; Ezek. 37:25). When preaching passages that speak of exiles returning to the land or the restoration of Zion's glory, we need to resist turning them into metaphors for the Church. Instead, affirm that God's faithfulness to Israel is the foundation on which Gentile salvation stands (Rom. 15:8-9).

2. Celebrate Gentile inclusion as a grafting-in, not a takeover.

The nations share the spiritual blessings of the New Covenant (Eph. 2:11-13), yet we do so as adopted children who honor the firstborn, Israel. Paul is very clear in Romans 11:11-24: the wild olive branches depend on the cultivated root, never the reverse.

3. Model mutual honor in worship and ministry.

Create space for Jewish followers of Jesus to hold on to *Torah*-shaped rhythms (Sabbath, the feasts, Hebrew blessings, etc.), while inviting Gentiles to bring their own cultural gifts. Unity grows best where our distinct callings are honored, not ignored or diluted (Acts 15; Gal. 2:7-9). A great idea would be to host a shared Passover meal led by Messianic Jews and then add testimonies from Gentiles of how they were saved by reading Israel's Scriptures and placing their faith in the Jewish Messiah.

4. Let prophetic hope energize present mission.

Because Israel's national resurrection (Ezek. 37) and the "latter rain" outpouring of the Holy Spirit on all flesh (Joel 2:23; cf.

vv.28-32) are certain, the Church can serve as the firstfruits of what is still to come – an end-time revival in Israel and the nations, and an ingathering of a harvest unlike anything seen before in history prior to the great day of YHWH. In the meantime, Jewish and Gentile believers in Messiah can partner for justice, mercy, and the proclamation of the gospel of the Kingdom.

I love Paul's words in Romans 11:15, where he highlights Israel's rejection of Jesus as their Messiah and their ultimate acceptance: "For if their rejection means the reconciliation of the world, what will their acceptance mean but life from the dead?" If you are a pastor or leader, keep that horizon before your people. Proclaim the coming day when Israel is restored in her land, the nations stream to Zion, and Messiah rules the earth. Teach them to live now as ambassadors of that future reality, honoring Israel's distinctive covenant and calling, while inviting all nations to rejoice in their Savior and King.

"It is too small a thing for you to be my servant
to restore the tribes of Jacob
and bring back those of Israel I have kept.
I will also make you a light for the nations,
that my salvation may reach to the ends of the earth."
(Isaiah 49:6 NIV)

Chapter 6

The Cross, the Covenant, and the Coming Kingdom

The crucifixion of Jesus is far more than the tragic death of a Jewish prophet. It is the fulfillment of Israel's story and the decisive turning point in human history. Through his death, Jesus enacts a new exodus, inaugurates the New Covenant, and sets in motion the final restoration of all things. This is not just abstract theology. It is firmly rooted in the biblical feasts, prophetic promises, and the enduring hope of Israel.

Jesus was crucified on the fourteenth day of the month Nisan, which is the day of Passover (cf. Matt. 26:2). Passover commemorates Israel's deliverance from slavery in Egypt (Exod. 12:6). That evening, the first day of the seven-day Feast of Unleavened Bread began (15-21 Nisan), during which Jesus was buried (Mark 15:42-46). In the Jewish way of counting, any part of a day was considered as a whole.[66] Therefore, Jesus' burial on Friday afternoon, his remaining in the tomb throughout the Sabbath (Saturday), and his resurrection early Sunday morning together count as three days. This fulfills Jesus' own prophecy that he would rise "on the third day" (Matt. 16:21; Luke 24:7). Unleavened Bread symbolizes the removal of impurity

---

[66] As explained by David Instone Brewer, "A day and a night (saith the tradition) make an Onah, and a part of an Onah is as the whole. ... The least part of the Onah concluded the whole." See:zDavid Instone Brewer, quoting the Babylonian Talmud in "What Did Jesus Mean by 'Three Days and Three Nights'?" Bible Archaeology, n.d., https://biblearchaeology.org/abr-projects/the-daniel-9-24-27-project-2/5134-what-did-jesus-mean-by-three-days-and-three-nights (accessed on August 21, 2025).

and separation from sin and points to the sinlessness of Messiah, who lay in the tomb during this time.

Jesus rose on the day after the Sabbath following Passover (Lev. 23:11), which corresponds to the Feast of Firstfruits (around 16-17 Nisan), when Israel brought the first sheaf of the harvest to God.[67] In this, Jesus fulfills the feast as the "firstfruits of those who have fallen asleep" (1 Cor. 15:20) and the "firstborn from the dead" (Col. 1:18). These feasts were not merely reminders of what God did in history but prophetic rehearsals of Messiah's redemptive work – both during his first and his second coming.

The Gospels – especially Matthew – deliberately cast Jesus' suffering as the fulfillment of Psalm 22. On the cross, Jesus utters the psalm's opening line: "My God, my God, why have you forsaken me?" (Matt. 27:46; cf. Ps. 22:1). Michael Heiser emphasizes the depth of this connection: "Matthew tracks on Psalm 22 in this description. The parallels are impossible to miss. ... Scholars have long noticed that elements of Psalm 22 appear to describe injuries and conditions congruent with crucifixion [esp. Ps. 22:14-15]."[68]

Indeed, the details align strikingly. Jesus is mocked and scorned. Bystanders wag their heads at him in derision. His hands and feet are pierced. Soldiers cast lots for his clothing. In weaving Psalm 22 into the passion narrative, Matthew underscores that Jesus'

---

67   See Leviticus 23:10–11: "...When you come into the land that I give you and reap its harvest, you shall bring the sheaf of the firstfruits of your harvest to the priest, and he shall wave the sheaf before the LORD, so that you may be accepted. On the day after the Sabbath the priest shall wave it." For the correlation between Jesus' resurrection and the Feast of Firstfruits, see e.g., Joe Turner, "Feast of First Fruits," EZTorah, https://eztorah.com/archive/feast-of-first-fruits/, accessed on Sept. 23, 2025. For the dating Nisan 16-17, see Richard Adu-Ntow, "Messiah in the Feast of First Fruits," *Jacob's Ladder Christian Fellowship*, 2024, on https://www.jacobsladdercf.org.uk/ teaching-articles/feast-of-first-fruits/messiah-in-the-feast-of-first-fruits, accessed on Sept. 23, 2025.

68   Michael S. Heiser, *The Unseen Realm*, 289.

suffering unfolds not as a tragic accident but in fulfillment of Israel's Scriptures.

Psalm 22 portrays not only physical agony but also spiritual conflict. "Strong bulls of Bashan surround me" (Ps. 22:12) may sound poetic but Heiser points out that Bashan was associated with cosmic evil and the realm of the dead.[69] Jesus' death on the cross is therefore not only a substitutionary sacrifice. It is the culmination of a cosmic battle in which Jesus, by his obedient suffering, disarms the powers of darkness (Col. 2:15) that had the nations in their grip.

In this light, Jesus is revealed as the ultimate Passover Lamb, not merely the one who delivers Israel from Pharaoh but the one who delivers all humanity from sin and death itself (1 Cor. 5:7). His resurrection on the Feast of Firstfruits marks the dawn of a new humanity, one that belongs to the age to come – the Messianic Age. And the unleavened bread of his sinless life becomes the sustaining nourishment of a covenant people made pure.

This pattern reinforces a central theme of restorationist theology: God has not abandoned the world, nor has he abandoned Israel. He is redeeming both. The death and resurrection of Jesus inaugurate the New Covenant, a covenant which will be fully realized when Jesus returns. Jesus' crucifixion and resurrection are not the nullification of Israel's prophetic feasts but their deepest realization.

The Resurrection and the Vindication of the Son

The resurrection of Jesus is not just a miracle. Through his resurrection, God demonstrates that Jesus is the true Messiah, the Son of God, and the firstborn of the new creation. The resurrection vindicates his identity, his mission and his message. Through it, the

---

69   Heiser, 289-290.

Father affirms that Jesus' death was not a failure, but the fulfillment of the covenant promises made to Israel.

Paul writes that Jesus "was declared to be the Son of God in power…by his resurrection from the dead" (Rom. 1:4). This is not a shift in his identity but a public unveiling of who he already was. In Jewish expectation, the resurrection was associated with the end of the age, the time when God would raise the righteous and restore Israel (cf. Dan. 12:2; Isa. 26:19). John Levenson asserts, "For the Jewish expectation of a resurrection of the dead is always and inextricably associated with the restoration of the people Israel; it is not, in the first instance, focused on individual destiny. The question it answers is not, 'Will I have life after death?' but rather, 'Has God given up on his promises to his people?'"[70] The answer to that last question is a resounding "No!" That the resurrection happened to one man, ahead of time, was unexpected but it confirmed that the age to come had already broken into the present age through Messiah.

The timing of Jesus' resurrection is again deeply significant. It occurred "on the first day of the week" (Matt. 28:1), which, according to Leviticus 23, coincided with the Feast of Firstfruits – the beginning of the barley harvest. This is when Israel brought the first portion of the crop to YHWH as a sign of the full harvest to come. Paul applies this imagery directly to Jesus: "Christ has been raised from the dead, the firstfruits of those who have fallen asleep" (1 Cor. 15:20). His resurrection is not the end of the story but the beginning of a greater ingathering. His resurrection is a promise that those who belong to him will likewise be raised. N. T. Wright expresses this hope powerfully: "The message of Easter is that God's

---

70   Jon D. Levenson, *Resurrection and the Restoration of Israel – The Ultimate Victory of the God of Life* (New Haven, CT: Yale University Press, 2006), 165.

new world has been unveiled in Jesus Christ and that you're now invited to belong to it."[71]

The resurrection is also the vindication of the suffering servant. Isaiah 53 does not end with defeat but with exaltation. When you translate 53:11-12 directly from the Hebrew, it says: "As a result of the anguish of his soul, he will see it and be satisfied. By his knowledge, the Righteous One, my Servant, will justify the many, as he will bear their iniquities. Therefore, I will allot him a portion with the great [or: the many] and he will divide the booty with the strong, because he poured out himself to death and was numbered with the transgressors. Yet he himself bore the sin of many and interceded for the transgressors." The suffering Servant's apparent defeat turned into history's greatest victory!

Psalm 22, which so clearly prophetically describes the crucifixion, also anticipates Jesus' vindication. After the darkness comes a turning point: "You have rescued me from the horns of the wild oxen!" (Ps. 22:21). The psalm then ends in global praise: "All the ends of the earth shall remember and turn to the LORD, and all the families of the nations shall worship before you. For kingship belongs to the LORD, and he rules over the nations" (Ps. 22:27-28). Jesus' death and resurrection form the fulcrum between despair and hope, suffering and glory. Jesus' death and resurrection fulfill the Psalm in its entirety, not only the cry of abandonment but also the triumphant conclusion. The resurrection confirms that Jesus' sacrifice was accepted and that the Servant has become the true King.

From a restorationist perspective, Jesus' resurrection is the dawning of the age to come, the beginning of the promised restoration of Israel and the renewal of the world. It is the seal on

---

71   N. T. Wright, *Surprised by Hope: Rethinking Heaven, the Resurrection, and the Mission of the Church* (New York: HarperCollins e-Books, 2008), 252-253.

the New Covenant, the first breath of the new creation. The King has been enthroned – not despite his suffering but because of it.

Jesus' Ascension and Enthronement

The resurrection is not the conclusion of Jesus' mission. Forty days after rising from the dead, he ascends into heaven – not to withdraw or retire from his redemptive work but to take his seat as the exalted Son of Man. His ascension marks the beginning of his heavenly reign and anticipates the fulfillment of the hope declared in Psalm 110: "The LORD says to my Lord: 'Sit at my right hand until I make your enemies your footstool'" (v.1).

Jesus' ascension, described in Acts 1:9-11, is not an escape from the earth but a royal procession. He is "taken up" into the clouds, evoking Daniel's apocalyptic vision: "Behold, with the clouds of heaven there came one like a son of man... and to him was given dominion and glory and a kingdom" (Dan. 7:13-14). Some interpreters – most notably N. T. Wright – understand Daniel's vision as a direct reference to Jesus' ascension, emphasizing that the "coming of the Son of Man" is a heavenly approach to the Ancient of Days rather than a descent to earth. While this reading highlights the exaltation aspect of the ascension, the broader context of Daniel 7 points beyond that moment, looking ahead to Messiah's return, when his dominion will be manifest, visible, and universal here on earth.

N. T. Wright emphasizes that Jesus has already been exalted as the Son of Man: "He is already risen. He is already, as a bodily human being, exalted into the presence of God. He is already ruling the world, not simply in some divine capacity but precisely as a human being."[72] He rightly highlights the reality of Jesus' present

---

72   N. T. Wright, "Early Traditions and the Origins of Christianity," originally published in *Sewanee Theological Review* 41.2, 1998. Available online at https://ntwrightpage.

enthronement as Messiah who reigns as a human being in heaven. Yet Wright's eschatology leans too heavily toward the "already" and too lightly on the "not yet." If Jesus' reign were fully realized now, why does evil still ravage the nations? Why do poverty, oppression, sickness, and death continue unchecked?

Scripture provides the answer: Jesus' reign is indeed real, but it remains veiled until the time of his return. As Peter preached in the temple courts, heaven must receive Christ "until the time for restoring all things" (Acts 3:21). The restoration of the kingdom to Israel is not a marginal appendix. It is central to God's cosmic renewal. The restoration has been inaugurated but it awaits completion. As Paul declares, Jesus "must reign until he has put all his enemies under his feet" (1 Cor. 15:25). Here the tension of "already and not yet" emerges with full force: the King is enthroned in heaven, yet the promises of Psalm 2 still reach forward. One day, he will return to Zion in glory to claim the nations as his inheritance: "As for me, I have set my King on Zion, my holy hill" (Ps. 2:6; cf. Ps. 2:8).

The New Covenant Ratified

Let us turn back the clock a few weeks from the Ascension to the Last Supper. What would the disciples have thought as Jesus spoke these startling words during that climactic Passover meal? "This cup that is poured out for you is the new covenant in my blood" (Luke 22:20). In a single sentence, he announced a moment pregnant with meaning. He was declaring that the long-awaited promise of Jeremiah 31:31-34 was about to be fulfilled.

At every Passover meal, four cups of wine were shared. When Jesus lifted the third cup – the cup of redemption – he redefined it in light of his own mission. His imminent death would inaugurate

---

com/2016/04/05/early-traditions-and-the-origins-of-christianity/, accessed on July 12, 2025.

the New Covenant. These were not abstract theological musings but a bold claim: the restoration of Israel was beginning in him. The biblical story was reaching its climax. Promises long deferred were now coming to fulfillment. The Kingdom was breaking in, and God's long-promised mercy was ready to flow to the nations through Israel's Messiah.

As with God's earlier covenants, the New Covenant was "cut" in blood (Gen. 15; Ex. 24). On Golgotha, Jesus poured out his life as the suffering Servant of Isaiah 53:12, securing the forgiveness of sins (Matt. 26:28) and restoring fellowship between God and his people. When the temple curtain was torn (Matt. 27:51), the way into God's presence was opened. The covenant was not merely proclaimed; it was inaugurated.

Yet the New Covenant promised more than forgiveness. It promised transformation: "I will put my law within them, and I will write it on their hearts" (Jer. 31:33). At Pentecost, that promise began to be fulfilled. The Spirit was poured out not just on prophets or priests but on all flesh – sons and daughters, old and young alike (Joel 2:28-29; Acts 2:17-18). What had once been inscribed on tablets of stone was now being etched on hearts of flesh (Ezek. 36:26-27; 2 Cor. 3:3). Obedience empowered through the Spirit became the distinguishing mark of the New Covenant community.

But watch this: the New Covenant would be made with the whole house of Israel and the house of Judah (Jer. 31:31). Verse 34 says that "they shall all know me, from the least of them to the greatest." Was that promise totally fulfilled on the day of Pentecost? No: the Spirit was poured out in Jerusalem on the disciples and other Jews, but Jeremiah's covenant was never only with Judah. It was with both houses. That is why Luke later records the Spirit coming upon the Samaritans (Acts 8), who represented the northern tribes.[73]

---

73   James T. Mace, *Ensign for the Nations*, 30-35. Mace argues that the Spirit's coming

In this way, the covenant promise unfolds in stages: first Judah in Jerusalem, then Israel's northern kin in Samaria, and then the nations to the ends of the earth.

The disciples in Jerusalem were only the firstfruits of a much larger harvest still to come. Paul makes clear in Romans 9-11 that much of Israel rejected Jesus as Messiah and hardened their hearts. Yet the story is not over. As Paul declares, "all Israel will be saved" (Rom. 11:26). These New Covenant promises are still pressing forward toward their fullness.

And what about the Gentiles? Only after Israel's divided house was being restored in Messiah did the covenant blessings begin to overflow to the nations (Acts 10-11). Non-Jewish believers are graciously included, not because they replace Israel but because they are united to Israel's Messiah and grafted into Israel's story (Rom. 11:17-24). This covenant does not erase Israel's national identity but upholds God's faithfulness to Israel (Rom. 11:29). Through Messiah, the blessing promised to Abraham's seed is extended to the nations (Gen. 12:3; Gal. 3:14) but never at Israel's expense. As Ariel Blumenthal asserts, reflecting on Ephesians 2: "But now, in Christ, ... the Gentile believer has become a full citizen and member of the household of God, no longer just an alien or stranger (*ger*) among Israel ... Now, for the first time in biblical history, the apostle can describe Israel as a 'commonwealth' (v.12) – a grouping of nations, each with its own unique identity, yet each with the full right of citizenship in the commonwealth as anyone from the 'mother' (central, original) nation of the commonwealth – Israel."[74]

And yet, the New Covenant lives in tension. It has been inaugurated but not yet consummated. Sins are forgiven (Heb.

---

upon Samaritans represents the reunification of Israel's divided houses (Judah and the northern tribes) in fulfillment of Jeremiah 31 and Ezekiel 37.

74   Ariel Blumenthal, *One New Man*, 109.

10:17-18), the Spirit has been given as a guarantee (Eph. 1:14) and the new creation has already broken in (2 Cor. 5:17). But full restoration – resurrection, renewed creation, and the visible reign of the King – is still to come (Rom. 8:23; 1 Cor. 15:22-26). The people of God live between the cross and the crown, empowered by the Spirit, living as a sacrifice, and longing for the full manifestation of the Kingdom. As the people of God, we live in the tension between his enthronement and his return – sharing in the mission of the King while awaiting the Day of YHWH. The Church does not build the Kingdom but bears witness to it. We do so through our proclamation, our works of love and our life together shaped by the sacraments – especially baptism and the Lord's Supper, which announces the death of the King "until he comes" (1 Cor. 11:26).

The ascension also secures Jesus' ongoing intercession. Seated at the right hand of the Father, he is our high priest who ever lives to intercede for his people (Heb. 7:25). His ascension does not create distance but ensures intimacy. He has entered the true heavenly temple "on our behalf" (Heb. 9:24), giving us confidence of both access and advocacy. The ascension is not an appendix to the gospel. It is the royal seal upon Jesus' finished work, the declaration that the crucified One now reigns as Lord. The restoration of all things has begun. In the meantime, we keep praying, "Your kingdom come, your will be done," until the King returns.

Pastoral Reflection: Covenant People in a Confused Age

The New Covenant is not merely a theological concept. It is the very air we breathe as followers of Jesus. We live in a world of broken promises, shattered identities, and empty covenants. In that world, we proclaim a Messiah who has upheld God's covenant with Israel, poured out his own blood for the forgiveness of sins, and given us his Spirit to empower us to live holy lives and be faithful witnesses.

As believers, we are not held together by programs or preferences but by the blood of the covenant. Each time we gather around the Lord's table, we are reminded that we belong to a story far greater than ourselves – a story stretching from Abraham to the first coming of Jesus, from Sinai to Zion, from a hill outside Jerusalem to a throne at the end of the age.

Our covenant life is not something abstract or distant but deeply practical. By the Spirit, God writes his *Torah* on our hearts, not to bind us in legalism but to form us in covenant loyalty. The New Covenant creates a new kind of humanity, marked by humility, holiness, and hope.

As pastors and leaders, our calling is to disciple people into that covenant identity. We are not merely conveying information. We are shaping lives. We invite people into rhythms of repentance and renewal, training them to recognize the voice of the Spirit. We guide them into obedience, not to earn salvation but to demonstrate it.

And we do this while holding fast to the mystery of God's unfolding plan. The covenant was made with Israel. As Gentile believers, we are wild branches grafted in by grace. That truth should produce humility, not pride, intercession, not indifference. For God is not finished with Israel – and he is not finished with the Church.

In a confused age marked by division, we must live as covenant people – anchored in the cross, filled with the Spirit, longing for the Kingdom, and faithful until the King returns. As we wait in hope and walk as covenant people, we pray with Jesus:

"Our Father in heaven,
hallowed be your name.
Your kingdom come,
your will be done,
on earth as it is in heaven.
Give us this day our daily bread,
and forgive us our debts,
as we also have forgiven our debtors.
And lead us not into temptation,
but deliver us from evil."
(Matthew 6:9-13)

Chapter 7

Pentecost and the Rebirth of the People of God

Pentecost was not the beginning of something entirely new. It was the fulfillment of a long-awaited promise, deeply rooted in Israel's sacred calendar. Known in Hebrew as *Shavuot*, the Feast of Weeks or Pentecost, this festival was celebrated fifty days after Passover and marked the firstfruits of the wheat harvest (Ex. 34:22; Lev. 23:15-21). In Jewish tradition, *Shavuot* also became associated with the giving of *Torah* at Mount Sinai.[75] It was a feast of covenant remembrance and covenant renewal.

So, when the Spirit is poured out in Acts 2, it is not some random divine intervention. It is a prophetic moment, perfectly timed. God chooses this feast, *Shavuot* – the day when Israel remembered its identity as a covenant people – to pour out his Spirit and begin the renewal of that very people. What took place at Sinai is now echoed in Jerusalem, on Mount Zion, only this time not on stone tablets but on human hearts (2 Cor. 3:3).

This is exactly what the prophets foresaw. Through Joel, God had promised: "I will pour out my Spirit on all flesh... your sons and your daughters shall prophesy... even on the male and female servants in those days I will pour out my Spirit" (Joel 2:28-29). Note

---

75 "Based on the Torah's description of when the Israelites arrived at Mount Sinai after the Exodus from Egypt (Exodus 19:1), the Rabbis set the date of the giving of the Torah as 6th day of the Hebrew month of Sivan, and the holiday that was once purely agricultural became the commemoration of the Israelites receiving the Torah at Mount Sinai." See "Shavuot History" on Reform Judaism, https://reformjudaism. org/jewish-holidays/shavuot/shavuot-history, accessed on July 13, 2025.

that the phrase "I will pour out my Spirit on all flesh" (Joel 2:28) is immediately followed by a list: "your sons and your daughters... your old men... your young men... even on the male and female servants." This literary structure suggests that Joel meant all segments of Judah's society, across gender, age, and social class. At this point, he was not speaking about the *goyim* – the Gentile nations.[76] Likewise, Ezekiel had prophesied that God would cleanse Israel, give them a new heart, and put his Spirit within them (Ezek. 36:25-27). And Jeremiah had spoken of a New Covenant, not a covenant with some unidentified future Church but explicitly "with the house of Israel and the house of Judah" (Jer. 31:31). This covenant was not a break from Israel's story but the continuation and renewal of it. *Torah* would not be cancelled but internalized: "I will put my law within them, and I will write it on their hearts" (Jer. 31:33). All these promises converge on *Shavuot*.

In this way, that day of Pentecost recorded in Acts 2 becomes a new Sinai but it's not a rejection of the old. It is the same God, renewing his covenant with his people in a deeper way. As the fire once descended on the mountain, it now descends on people. As the voice once thundered from the cloud, it is now heard through Spirit-filled witnesses speaking in many languages about the "mighty works of God" (Acts 2:11). The same God, the same people but now with a new heart and a new power.

God's timing is deliberate. Pentecost does not initiate a new religion. It was not the start of Christianity or the birth of the Church. It did mark the beginning of Israel's restoration through Messiah. That is why it happened in a Jewish city: Jerusalem, with Jewish disciples, on a Jewish feast day. The nations will be included

---

76   See David Allan Hubbard, *Joel and Amos, Tyndale Old Testament Commentaries,* vol. 25 (Downers Grove, IL: IVP Academic, 2009), 73.

– yes – but only later (Acts 10-11; 15). Restoration always begins at the root.

And what about the harvest? *Shavuot* was about firstfruits. In Acts 2, the 3,000 who respond in faith are the firstfruits of the New Covenant community. They are not a break from Israel's past but the beginning of its prophetic renewal. The Hebrew prophets had long spoken of a faithful remnant that would survive judgment and return to God (see Isa. 10:20-22). While that passage originally referred to a return from exile, its theology shaped the expectation that God would one day restore a core within Israel – a remnant of those who trust in him and respond in repentance. In Acts 2, we see such a remnant: Jewish disciples from all over the known world, responding to Messiah with repentance and faith. This is not the creation of a new people but the reconstitution of the *ekklesia*, the assembly of faithful Israelites, first seen in the Hebrew Bible (e.g. Deut. 4:10; Ps. 22:22). The Greek word *ekklesia* is the same word used in the Septuagint to translate *qahal*, the assembly at Sinai. The Holy Spirit's outpouring does not birth something foreign to Israel's identity. It revives it.

Even the number 3,000 carries prophetic weight. When Israel broke the covenant at Sinai by worshiping the golden calf, about 3,000 men died that day (Ex. 32:28). Now, at this new and better Sinai – Mount Zion in Jerusalem – 3,000 receive life and are added to the New Covenant community. What the law written on stone could not accomplish, the Spirit now begins to fulfill. Instead of judgment, he brings transformation.

The Spirit Poured Out in Jerusalem

Shavuot (Pentecost) did not take place in a spiritual vacuum. It unfolded in Jerusalem, the covenant city, where the temple was located and where God said he would cause his name to dwell. This is not by accident. The restoration of Israel had long been associated with a renewal that would be centered in Zion. "Out of Zion shall go the law, and the word of the LORD from Jerusalem" (Isa. 2:3). So, when the Spirit is poured out in Acts 2, it is not an abstract empowerment for personal experience. It is a covenantal act, a prophetic fulfillment, and a geographical signal that restoration is beginning at the root.

The crowd that gathered was made up of devout Jews "from every nation under heaven" (Acts 2:5). This was not yet a Gentile Pentecost. These were Jews living in the diaspora, faithful to the God of Israel, who gathered in Jerusalem as pilgrims for *Shavuot* in obedience to Deuteronomy 16:16: "Three times a year all your males shall appear before the LORD your God at the place that he will choose: at the Feast of Unleavened Bread, at the Feast of Weeks [*Shavuot* / Pentecost], and at the Feast of Booths. They shall not appear before the LORD empty-handed."[77] *Shavuot* is one of the *mo'edim* (appointed times), one of those moments God wanted to meet with his people. From all over the world, they had come to Jerusalem, the city of the Great King. And it was here that the Lord met them, launching a renewal that would ripple out to Jewish communities across the Roman Empire.

After Pentecost, these diaspora Jews would return to their homelands, bringing with them the message of the gospel and news about the long-awaited Messiah. In this way, the firstfruits gathered in Jerusalem became messengers to their own communities, giving

---

77 See also Exodus 23:14-17. Notice how they had to "appear before the LORD your God at the place that he will choose" (Deut. 16:16). When the Israelites received this command at Sinai, they did not yet know that this place would be Jerusalem. Later Scripture and Jewish tradition clearly identify Jerusalem as that chosen place. 2 Sam.6 shows that the ark is moved to Jerusalem and in 1 Kings 8 we can see that the temple is established in Jerusalem. Psalm 122:3-4 says: "Jerusalem – built as a city that is bound firmly together, to which the tribes go up, the tribes of the LORD, as was decreed for Israel, to give thanks to the name of the Lord. By the Second Temple period (including the time of Jesus), pilgrimage to Jerusalem for *Shavuot* was a well-established custom based on these commands. This explains why Acts 2 describes devout Jews from "every nation under heaven" gathered in Jerusalem.

Jews throughout the diaspora the opportunity to hear and respond. So, they too could join the ranks of those firstfruits of the renewed covenant people.[78]

Among those gathered in Jerusalem, the apostles themselves were also thoroughly Jewish. They were not representatives of a new religious movement but members of the faithful remnant of Israel who were waiting for their national redemption. Their faith in Jesus did not make them less Jewish than before they met Jesus. On the contrary, it intensified their longing for Israel's restoration. Luke tells us that before Pentecost – after Jesus had taught them about the Kingdom for another forty days (Acts 1:3) – they asked: "Lord, will you at this time restore the kingdom to Israel?" (Acts 1:6). Jesus didn't correct them. He just challenged their sense of timing: "It is not for you to know times or seasons that the Father has fixed by his own authority" (Acts 1:7). And then he promised them the power of the Holy Spirit, so they would be effective witnesses to the Kingdom "in Jerusalem and in all Judea and Samaria, and to the end of the earth" (Acts 1:8).

So Acts chapter 2 describes the outpouring of the Holy Spirit in Jerusalem, fulfilling the prophetic words spoken centuries earlier. Through Joel, God had promised: "I will pour out my Spirit on all flesh" (Joel 2:28). As we saw earlier, this "all flesh" was not a reference to the Gentiles but to all Israel, sons and daughters, old and young, servants and free. The covenant community of Israel would be revived from within.[79]

---

78   See Acts 2:5-11 for the extensive list of diaspora Jewish communities present at Pentecost. Scholars widely recognize that these pilgrims, after experiencing the outpouring of the Spirit in Jerusalem, would have returned home and become among the earliest witnesses to their home synagogues, helping spread the gospel throughout the Jewish world.

79   See David Allan Hubbard, *Joel and Amos*, 73. Hubbard notes that Joel's "all flesh" refers contextually to "all Israel – sons and daughters, old and young, servants and free," not Gentile nations.

The same train of thought can be found in Ezekiel's vision: "I will sprinkle clean water on you, and you shall be clean... I will give you a new heart, and a new spirit I will put within you" (Ezek. 36:25-26). This is spoken not to the Church but to the house of Israel (Ezek. 36:22). Similarly, the New Covenant promised in Jeremiah is "with the house of Israel and the house of Judah" (Jer. 31:31). The New Covenant is not about abandoning *Torah* but about internalizing it: "I will put my law within them, and I will write it on their hearts" (Jer. 31:33).[80] These prophetic texts all converge on Jerusalem at Pentecost.

The setting matters. The temple was the symbol of God's presence, the heart of Israel's national identity. And now, instead of fire descending on a mountain or filling a tabernacle, tongues of fire rest on a people, on the descendants of Abraham, Isaac, and Jacob. God is again taking up residence with his people but this time in a way that points ahead to a greater fulfillment. This is not the final outpouring promised in the prophets, only its firstfruits – a downpayment of what is to come when God pours out "a spirit of grace and pleas for mercy" upon the house of David and the inhabitants of Jerusalem (Zech. 12:10). The Holy Spirit is not launching a new religion. He is breathing life into the dry bones of Israel's hope. The prophets had spoken of a remnant, a faithful core who would return to God in the last days (Isa. 10:20-22). Now, in Jerusalem, that remnant is being formed. It is the beginning of restoration – but the nations have not yet come in. First, the house of Israel must be revived.

---

80 Both Ezekiel 36 and Jeremiah 31 specify that covenant renewal and the giving of the Spirit are for the house of Israel. These texts should form the backbone of any New Covenant expectation.

Peter's Sermon and the Reconstitution of Israel

When the Spirit is poured out and the crowd gathers, Peter gets up to preach. His message is not a random motivational speech. It is the Spirit-filled voice of a Jewish disciple interpreting the Scriptures in light of what had just happened. Peter's sermon is saturated with the Hebrew Bible. He begins with Joel, moves to Psalms, and climaxes with a declaration that Jesus is both "Lord and Messiah" (Acts 2:36). This is not merely good theology. Peter explains what restoration looks like. Peter is reinterpreting Israel's sacred texts around the crucified and risen Jesus. In doing so, he is calling the people of Israel to recognize their long-awaited *Mashiach*, their Messianic King.

Peter begins by addressing the prophetic significance of the moment. "This is what was uttered through the prophet Joel," he says, quoting the promise that God would pour out his Spirit "on all flesh" (Acts 2:16-17). As we saw earlier, Joel's vision was not initially about Gentiles receiving an outpouring of the Holy Spirit but about Judah's own sons, daughters, old men, and servants. The Spirit's outpouring in Acts 2 is therefore not the fulfillment of a new plan but the continuation of the prophetic story: a covenant people being revived by God's own breath, God's own Spirit.

He then shifts to David and the Psalms, especially Psalm 16 and Psalm 110. David, Peter argues, spoke of the resurrection and exaltation of Messiah. Jesus has fulfilled what David foresaw. He is not only Israel's crucified servant but also the risen Son, seated at God's right hand. The crowd is "cut to the heart" (Acts 2:37). Peter continues with a simple and radical invitation: "Repent and be baptized every one of you in the name of Jesus Christ [=Messiah] for the forgiveness of your sins, and you will receive the gift of the Holy Spirit" (Acts 2:38).

This call to baptism would not have sounded foreign to Peter's Jewish listeners. Ritual immersion (*tevilah*) was a familiar practice

101

in Second Temple Judaism – used for purification, covenant renewal, and initiation into various Jewish sects. John the Baptizer had already introduced an immersion of repentance and allegiance, preparing hearts for the coming Kingdom. *Mikva'ot* (ritual baths) were plentiful throughout the temple complex.[81] Immersion was more than a private act of cleansing. It was a visible sign of allegiance to the God of Israel and a demonstration of return to covenant faithfulness. Now, in light of Jesus' resurrection, this practice becomes a public declaration that Jesus is Israel's promised Messiah. What had long served as a demonstration of repentance and covenant loyalty is transformed into a personal identification with – and allegiance to – the crucified and risen King, showing prophetic participation in the renewal of Israel.

Yet this embrace comes at a cost. Repentance (*teshuvah*) is not merely emotional remorse. It means a decisive break from old loyalties, whether corrupt temple leadership, collusion with Roman imperial power, or misplaced nationalistic hopes. So, baptism in the name of Jesus is more than a private ritual or mere symbol. It is a public declaration of allegiance to the King – a burial of the old identity and a resurrection into the life of the New Covenant.[82]

Only then, through repentance and immersion, are they promised the gift of the Holy Spirit. The Spirit is not a spiritual accessory. He is the power of the New Covenant, the breath of Israel's renewed life. He empowers obedience, ignites witness, and transforms the *ekklesia* from within.

Luke concludes the account by noting that "about three thousand souls were added that day" (Acts 2:41). This number is deeply symbolic. As we saw earlier, it echoes the day Israel broke

---

81   Meir Ben-Dov, *In the Shadow of the Temple* (New York: HarperCollins, 1985), 152.

82   On baptism as transfer of allegiance, see Matthew Bates, *Salvation by Allegiance Alone* (Grand Rapids, MI: Baker Academic, 2017), esp. chapter 9.

the covenant at Sinai, when about 3,000 perished in judgment (Ex. 32:28). Now, at this renewed Sinai in Jerusalem, 3,000 receive life. This moment marks a prophetic reversal: judgment is replaced by renewal, as the Spirit breathes life into a remnant that will carry the covenant forward.

The outpouring of the Holy Spirit in Acts 2 does not inaugurate a new religion. Rather, it marks the reconstitution of Israel around its Messiah. The Pentecost story is not a departure from Israel's story but its fulfillment, a moment when God revives a faithful remnant from within Israel itself. The Spirit breathes fresh life into the ancient covenant community – the *qahal* – anticipating the day when the nations, too, will be gathered into this renewed assembly.

From Sinai to Zion

The book of Acts is about so much more than the birth of a movement. It unveils the rebirth of a covenant people. What happened at Sinai is now echoed on Mount Zion in Jerusalem. The *ekklesia* of Messiah is not a new religious entity but the revived *qahal* – the restored assembly of Israel through the Spirit.

At Sinai, the people trembled before a mountain wrapped in fire and smoke. At Zion, the fire comes down again. Now, it doesn't rest on a mountain but on a people. Just as God's presence once filled the tabernacle (Exod. 40:34-35) and later the temple (1 Kings 8:10-11), now his presence fills his people. They themselves become the new dwelling place of God (Eph. 2:22).

This shift was not unforeseen. Jeremiah had prophesied of a day when *Torah* would no longer be external, etched on stone tablets but written on human hearts (Jer. 31:33). What Moses longed for – "Would that all the LORD's people were prophets" (Num. 11:29) – now begins to unfold in the Spirit-filled and Spirit-empowered community.

The description in Acts 2:42-47 paints a vivid portrait of this renewed covenant community: steadfast devotion to the apostles' teaching, shared meals, radical generosity, and a life shaped by prayer. The inner transformation brought about by the Spirit manifested in public holiness and profound social solidarity. This is the kind of communal life God envisioned for the *qahal* when he gave Israel the *Torah* at Sinai. The "old" covenant was not set aside; it was internalized, deepened, and would now animate the entire community.

As we saw earlier in this chapter, the concepts of *qahal* and *ekklesia* were not new inventions that were introduced in Acts 2. The *qahal* – the assembly gathered at Sinai (Deut. 4:10; cf. Ps. 22:22) – is continued in the reconstituted *ekklesia* in Acts – now centered around Messiah Jesus.

And note the location: Jerusalem, the city where the name of YHWH dwelled, becomes the launchpad of a greater restoration which will take place when Jesus returns. From Mount Zion the *Torah* was to go forth (Isa. 2:3). And, so it does, not merely on scrolls but now in Spirit-filled witnesses upon whose hearts *Torah* has been inscribed. The *qahal* is alive!

The Samaritans are Invited Back into the Family of Israel

The Spirit's outpouring at Pentecost was only the beginning of Israel's restoration, and not its completion. While the first to receive the Spirit were Jews gathered in Jerusalem, the promise of the Father was never meant to stop there. From the very beginning, God had declared that his covenant with Abraham would be a blessing to all nations (Gen. 12:3).[83] Now, through Messiah, the door begins to open.

---

83   Genesis 12:3 establishes the foundational covenant with Abraham: "In you all the families of the earth shall be blessed." This promise is later echoed in Acts 3:25 and

But the inclusion of the nations doesn't happen all at once. It follows a carefully ordered progression: Jerusalem, Judea, Samaria, and then the ends of the earth (Acts 1:8). This is not accidental. God is restoring the nations in stages, starting with the whole house of Israel, and at each major turning point, he confirms the work of the Spirit through the presence of the apostles from Jerusalem, those who had walked with Jesus during his ministry on earth.

The first major step beyond Jerusalem and Judea takes place in Samaria (Acts 8:4-25). The Samaritans, regarded by most Jews as ethnically mixed and religiously compromised, were historically viewed with deep suspicion and even contempt. Yet, as James T. Mace points out, the Samaritans also saw themselves – and were seen by some – as descendants of the northern tribes, the house of Israel. Their inclusion is thus far more than an outreach to a fringe group. It is a prophetic sign of Israel's reunification under the New Covenant.[34]

When Philip preaches the gospel in Samaria, many believe and are baptized but the Holy Spirit does not fall on them until Peter and John arrive from Jerusalem and lay hands on them (Acts 8:14-17). This delay is theologically significant: God withholds his Spirit until the apostles themselves can personally affirm and embrace the Samaritans. What occurs is not simply the validation of a new ethnic group. It is the apostolic recognition that those once considered outsiders – who in reality represent the lost northern kingdom – are now fully restored to covenant fellowship with Judah, recalling the days of David's and Solomon's unified kingdom. This unification

---

Galatians 3:8, where it is interpreted as the gospel extended to the nations.

84   Mace, *Ensign for the Nations*, esp. 29-41. Mace traces the development of the early church's mission in Acts and highlights the distinct dynamics of the Samaritan mission as compared to the Gentile mission. He argues convincingly that the Samaritans represent the remnant of the northern kingdom, so their inclusion in the ekklesia signals the beginning of the restoration of the house of Israel.

prefigures the prophetic hope of Ezekiel 37, where the "two sticks" of Judah and Israel are joined as one.

Significantly, the Acts 8 narrative does not mention the outward signs associated with other outpourings of the Spirit. There is no record of tongues, prophecy, or dramatic manifestations as in Acts 2 (the Jewish Pentecost) or Acts 10-11 (the Gentile outpouring upon Cornelius and his household). Instead, Luke's account centers exclusively on the apostles' laying on of hands. This act functions as a public, apostolic welcome, reintegrating the Samaritans as full members of the covenant community and as firstfruits in the restoration of all Israel. The focus is not on charismatic signs but on reconciliation and reunification within God's unfolding work of prophetic restoration.

Thus, the Samaritan Pentecost is not the beginning of a separate movement but the restoration and the renewal of the *ekklesia*. And, crucially, it marks the return of the lost northern tribes into the family of Israel. The laying on of hands by Peter and John is a prophetic demonstration: a visible, authoritative embrace of the Samaritans back into the covenant, showing that the house of Israel is being restored, stage by stage, exactly as the prophets foretold.

The Nations Begin to Join

The next turning point comes in Acts 10, with Cornelius, a Roman centurion and "God-fearer." Here, too, God takes the initiative. He sends an angel to Cornelius and gives a vision to Peter. When Peter arrives, he preaches Jesus as Lord and Messiah. Before Peter finishes his message, "the Holy Spirit fell on all who heard the word" (Acts 10:44). This surprises even the people who were with Peter: "the gift of the Holy Spirit was poured out even on the Gentiles" (v.45). Luke deliberately creates a parallel between this scene and the original outpouring on the Jewish disciples in Acts 2. These Gentiles are then baptized, not as proselytes to Judaism but as full participants in the New Covenant as Gentiles. The Spirit includes them without conversion to Jewish identity. They are grafted in as Gentiles, not as Jews (Rom. 11:17-24).

This Gentile Pentecost is so controversial that Peter had to defend it before the leaders in Jerusalem. In Acts 11, he recounts the whole episode: the angel, the vision, and the Spirit's outpouring. He concludes, "If then God gave the same gift to them as he gave to us when we believed in the Lord Jesus Christ, who was I that I could stand in God's way?" (Acts 11:17). All the leaders of the Jerusalem church eventually agree: "Then to the Gentiles also God has granted repentance that leads to life" (Acts 11:18).

This affirmation is further solidified in Acts 15, at the Jerusalem Council. While this pivotal chapter deserves deeper exploration later on in this book, we must at least note here that it is a formal validation of what had begun in Acts 10. The apostles and elders agree: Gentiles are being included in the restored people of God without first having to become Jews. James, loosely quoting Amos 9:11-12 from the Septuagint, declares that the fallen tent of David is being rebuilt so "that the remnant of mankind may seek the Lord, and all the Gentiles who are called by my name" (Acts 15:17). This is not replacement. It is an expansion. The tent is being stretched but Israel remains the foundation.

When the Spirit is poured out on Samaritans and Gentiles it is not a sign that Israel's identity has been set aside. Rather, it is a confirmation that Israel's calling – to be a light to the nations – is being fulfilled in and through Messiah. With each widening circle of inclusion, God affirms this unfolding restoration by giving the same sign: the gift of the Holy Spirit. What emerges is not a new religion but the fulfillment of what the prophets foretold long ago.

Spiritual Gifts and the Empowered Remnant

The outpouring of the Holy Spirit at Pentecost is not just a sign. It is a surge of divine power. The same Spirit who hovered over the waters at creation now fills God's people, breathing life into dry bones and equipping them for mission. What emerges in Jerusalem is not a passive group of believers but an awakened remnant, called to witness, serve, and embody the restoration promised by the prophets. The prophetic promises no longer linger in shadows; they are now activated and visible: "Your sons and your daughters shall prophesy... your young men shall see visions, and your old men shall dream dreams" (Acts 2:17; cf. Joel 2:28).

Spiritual gifts become the tangible evidence of this supernatural empowerment. Gifts that were once only given to prophets, priests, and kings are now democratized – made available to all. The Spirit is poured out, not just on elite leaders but on ordinary men and women, young and old, even on servants. The fire of Sinai was no longer confined to a mountain or a tabernacle. It now rests on a people.

Some of these spiritual gifts, like the ones listed in Romans 12, reflect natural abilities, such as teaching, leadership, and generosity, now anointed with supernatural grace. Others, like the "grace gifts" (*charismata*) in 1 Corinthians 12, come as sudden flashes of divine initiative: prophecy, healing, discernment, tongues. These are not earned or mastered but bestowed by the Spirit as he wills to anyone, Jew or Gentile, according to the need of the moment. These spiritual gifts demonstrate the powers of the age to come in our present, broken world, and point to the coming King. They testify that the same God, who once poured out his Spirit on the prophets of old, is now equipping a restored people to carry his light to the ends of the earth. As the Apostle Paul said: "To each is given the manifestation of the Spirit for the common good" (1 Cor. 12:7).

The Book of Acts gives several glimpses of ministry empowered by the Holy Spirit. Peter preaches boldly, quoting the Hebrew Bible with authority. Stephen, "full of grace and power," performs signs and wonders (Acts 6:8). Agabus prophesies about a famine (Acts 11:28). Philip's daughters are described as prophetesses (Acts 21:9). The restored *ekklesia* is not a passive gathering but a living, active Body marked by supernatural gifts.

The Ephesians 4 gift list (apostles, prophets, evangelists, pastors, and teachers) is a bit different, and their role, as we head toward the restoration of all things, will be discussed more in-depth in a later chapter. For now, it is important to mention that these five expressions of leadership are not ecclesiastical titles or ranks. They are Messiah's gifts to his Body, given "to equip the saints for the work of ministry, for building up the body of Christ" (Eph. 4:11-12). Their ultimate purpose is unity and maturity "until we all attain to the unity of the faith and of the knowledge of the Son of God" (v.13). From a restorationist perspective this is deeply significant. The fivefold ministry is not a New Testament invention but a messianic continuation of Israel's leadership offices. Apostles mirror Moses' role as "sent ones."[85] Prophets carry on the tradition of the seers who called Israel to covenant faithfulness. Evangelists carry Isaiah's good news of a King who will reign from Zion and will establish peace (Isa. 52:7). Pastors reflect David's shepherd's heart on behalf of the Great Shepherd, and teachers propagate the wisdom of *Torah* (meaning "instruction") to God's people.

What is important to see is that these gifts of the Spirit are not optional extras. They are the means by which God restores his people and equips them for their calling. They are the tools of the remnant – those who respond to Messiah with repentance and

---

85   The Hebrew for "apostle" is *shaliach* (pl. *shlichim*), which means "emissary." Fun fact: a pizza delivery guy in Hebrew is called a *shaliach pizza*, a "pizza apostle."

faith. This is what sets the restored *ekklesia* apart: Spirit-empowered witness and love, not just theological accuracy or higher ethics.

The same Spirit who raised Jesus from the dead now dwells in his people (Rom. 8:11). The same power that parted the Red Sea is now at work in the Body of Messiah. We are not waiting for restoration to begin. It has begun. But we are waiting for its consummation. And in the meantime, the gifts of the Holy Spirit empower us to bear witness to the coming King and his Kingdom, build up the Body, and anticipate the day when "the earth will be filled with the knowledge of the glory of the LORD as the waters cover the sea" (Hab. 2:14).

Pastoral Reflection: A Spirit-Filled People Awaiting the Full Harvest

Pentecost was not a conclusion. It was a beginning: a firstfruits offering to God and a signpost for what is yet to come. When the Spirit descended in wind and fire, he did far more than launch a movement. He awakened a people. Those early believers in Jerusalem were not detached from God's past work. They were part of a developing story: a prophetic remnant, stirred by the breath of God, rooted in the covenant promises to Israel, and empowered for global mission.

We are part of that same Spirit-filled people: a community that did not replace Israel but that joins itself to her calling, shaped by the Jewish Messiah who fulfills the Law and prophets. Paul's image of Gentiles being grafted into God's cultivated olive tree (Rom. 11:17-24) reminds us of a sacred partnership: one Body, many members; one harvest, many fields. And yet, the harvest is not complete.

We live in the tension of the now and the not yet. The Spirit has been given as a firstfruits. The Kingdom of God has begun to break in. And gifts are being poured out in anticipation of the consummation that is still to come. Still, we wait. We long for the day when, as the prophets foretold, Israel's fullness will bring life from the dead (Rom. 11:15), and all nations will stream to the mountain of the LORD (Isa. 2:2). Pentecost was the down payment. The full harvest, when every tribe, tongue, and nation will honor the Lord, is still to come. So how do we live in this time in-between?

1. As a Renewed People.
We are not just individuals saved from sin but a Spirit-formed community, shaped by Scripture, sacraments, generosity, shared mission, and prophetic vision. We embody God's future restoration in the present: living as signs of what will be in a world that is still hurting.

2. With Gratitude for Israel.
Our faith is not disconnected from its roots. We honor Israel not merely as history but as God's covenant people, through whom Messiah came and to whom Messiah will return. We pray for her peace. We long for her fullness. And we remember that our own inclusion is an act of mercy of the God of Israel himself.

3. By Walking in the Spirit.
The same Spirit who hovered over the deep in Genesis now leads us daily, prompting us to bear fruit, discern truth, pursue justice, and offer comfort. Spiritual gifts are not badges of honor. They are tools for service and signs that the powers of the age to come are already at work among us.

4. Longing for Restoration.
We live in the tension of joy and pain, celebrating what God has already done, and yearning for what will still be revealed. We pray, "Maranatha, come, Lord Jesus," not as an escape but as hopeful

anticipation of the healing of the nations, the reconciliation of Jew and Gentile, and the restoration of all things.

In the end, being a Spirit-filled people is not about walking in God's power alone. It is about presence: God dwelling among his people, shaping us into a holy community for the sake of a broken world. We are not merely waiting. We are preparing. We are embodying. We are pointing forward. A great harvest is coming!

"For the earth will be filled with the knowledge of the glory of the LORD as the waters cover the sea."
(Habakkuk 2:14)

Chapter 8

The Mystery Revealed: One New Man in Messiah

When Paul writes about the "mystery of Christ" in Ephesians 3, he is not referring to something mysterious in the modern sense – unknowable or obscure. In Jewish apocalyptic thought, a "mystery" (*mustērion*) was a divine purpose long hidden but now made known through revelation.[86] The mystery is not that Gentiles could be saved – that was already anticipated in the Hebrew Scriptures – but the manner of their inclusion.

Paul explains that this mystery was "not made known to the sons of men in other generations as it has now been revealed to his holy apostles and prophets by the Spirit" (Eph. 3:5). So, what is new is not that Gentiles can be saved but that they are "fellow heirs, members of the same body, and partakers of the promise in Christ Jesus through the gospel" (v.6). This is radical: Gentiles are included as Gentiles, without needing to convert to Judaism. They become part of the covenant community through union with Messiah, not through circumcision, *Torah*-keeping, or national affiliation.

Paul presents the *ekklesia* as the renewed people of God – a covenant community brought together through Messiah. This Body consists of a Jewish remnant (the Old Testament *qahal*) and believing Gentiles who are grafted in (Rom. 11:17), all joined by the same Spirit

---

86   Christopher Rowland and Christopher R.A. Morray-Jones, *The Mystery of God: Early Jewish Mysticism and the New Testament*, CRINT 12 (Leiden: Brill, 2009), 123.

into one unified Body. Here, unity is grounded in a shared covenantal calling and mission, rather than in cultural or ethnic sameness.

Paul's calling was to steward this mystery "for the sake of you Gentiles" (Eph. 3:1 NIV). His apostolic commission was far more than merely spreading a simplified version of the gospel. It was to articulate, embody, and champion the profound reality of God's multi-ethnic family centered on Israel's Messiah. Paul's deep passion for the unity of Jew and Gentile in Messiah saturates his letters and stands at the heart of his theology of the restored *ekklesia*.

The mystery that Paul writes about reveals God's age-old plan. As he says elsewhere, "this was according to the eternal purpose that he has realized in Christ Jesus our Lord" (Eph. 3:11). The plan was always to unite heaven and earth, Israel and the nations, through Messiah – not by erasing distinctions but by reconciling them.[87]

The New Humanity in Ephesians 2:11-22

Paul does not envision a "third race" when describing the "one new man" or "one new humanity" in Ephesians 2 but a reconciled community grounded in Israel's promises and centered on Messiah.[88] Gentiles, once "separated from Christ, alienated from the commonwealth of Israel and strangers to the covenants of promise" (Eph. 2:12), are now "brought near by the blood of Christ" (v.13). They are not simply added to a new universal people of God but are grafted into Israel's covenantal story. So, the "one new man" is not a third race, nor does it negate the prior identities of Jew and Gentile. Instead, it signals the creation of a renewed reality in which both

---

87   Romans 15:8-9 supports this idea: "Christ became a servant to the circumcised... in order that the Gentiles might glorify God for his mercy."

88   For an extensive discussion on why Paul did not have a "third race" in mind when writing Ephesians, see Andrew R. Rillera, "Tertium Genus or Dyadic Unity? Investigating Sociopolitical Salvation in Ephesians," *Biblical Research* 66 (2021): 31-51, https://digitalcommons.georgefox.edu/cgi/viewcontent.cgi?article=1061&context=dmin (accessed on 23 Nov. 2025).

are reconciled in the Messiah without losing their distinct callings. Gentile believers are brought into Israel's ongoing covenantal story – not as a replacement for Israel or as a separate people but as participants in the fulfillment of Israel's promises through Messiah.

Jesus is "our peace," not by erasing ethnic or covenantal distinctions but by destroying the enmity that separated Jew and Gentile. Paul writes that Messiah "has broken down in his flesh the dividing wall of hostility" (Eph. 2:14-15). This likely alludes both to the *soreg* (the physical barrier in the Jerusalem temple that prohibited Gentiles from entering the inner courts under threat of death) and to the social and covenantal boundary created by the *Torah's* commandments and ordinances, which marked out Israel's distinct identity among the nations.[89] Yet Jesus does not cancel Israel's covenant calling. Instead, he fulfills *Torah* and removes it as a barrier between peoples, writing its intent on the hearts of those who belong to him (Jer. 31:33; Rom. 8:4).

The inclusion of Samaritans in Acts 8 is pivotal in this unfolding restoration, as we saw earlier. Far from being a side note, it signifies the re-gathering of the northern tribes, historically estranged from Judah, into one covenant community. The apostolic affirmation of Samaritan believers – through the laying on of hands – serves as a prophetic act, demonstrating the reunification of Israel as envisioned by Ezekiel and anticipated by Jesus. This Samaritan inclusion represents a critical turning point, as we saw earlier: it prophetically anticipates the ultimate gathering of all Israel's

---

89   The *soreg* inscription warned Gentiles not to pass beyond a certain point in the temple on pain of death. See Christopher Eames, "The Temple Warning Inscriptions: 'Closest Thing to the Temple We Have,'" *Armstrong Institute of Biblical Archaeology*, August 1, 2021, https://www.armstronginstitute.org/360-the-temple-warning-inscriptions-closest-thing-to-the-temple-we-have (accessed on 24 November 2025). On the *Torah's* boundary-marking role, see James D. G. Dunn, *The New Perspective on Paul*, revised ed. (Grand Rapids: Eerdmans, 2008), esp. p.52, which deals with Ephesians 2.

scattered tribes and foreshadows the later, full inclusion of the Gentiles into God's covenant family.

Building on this restoration, Paul describes the plan, which is to create "one new man in place of the two, so making peace" (Eph. 2:15). This "one new man" is not a generic Christian identity but the renewed people of God – Israel restored and enlarged to include both the faithful Jewish remnant and believing Gentiles. Gentile inclusion does not erase Israel's unique role. Instead, Gentiles are grafted into Israel's covenant story and warned against arrogance: "it is not you who support the root, but the root that supports you" (Rom. 11:18).

Sadly, two Gentile attitudes toward Israel and the Jewish people have been very common throughout history: jealousy, when God's covenant faithfulness to Israel is viewed with resentment, and arrogance, when the nations assume they have replaced Israel or believe they are superior. Both attitudes are rebuked in Scripture and are contrary to God's purpose. Instead, Gentile believers are called to humility, gratitude, and partnership in the promises given to Israel's patriarchs (Eph. 3:6; Rom. 11:11, 20-21).[90] So, Paul's vision is not a hybrid or disconnected identity, but a reconstituted *ekklesia*: the Spirit-filled *qahal* now enlarged to include the nations. Gentile believers do not replace Israel but are joined to God's existing covenant family, becoming "fellow citizens with the saints and members of the household of God" (Eph. 2:19).

Paul further explains that this new humanity is "built on the foundation of the apostles and prophets, Christ Jesus himself being the cornerstone" (Eph. 2:20). While some see "apostles and prophets" here as purely New Testament figures, others argue that the phrase refers to a continuity of witness from the Hebrew prophets (the *Tanakh*) to the apostolic message of the gospel.

---

90   On Gentile jealousy and arrogance, see especially Paul's warnings in Rom. 11:11-25.

However, Eph. 3:5 clarifies that the mystery of Messiah "has now been revealed to his holy apostles and prophets by the Spirit." This supports the interpretation that these are New Covenant prophets working alongside the apostles. So, the *ekklesia* is rooted in fresh apostolic-prophetic revelation, with Jesus as its defining center. Yet its foundation stands firmly on the story of Israel, rather than diverging from it.

Jesus is the cornerstone (Eph. 2:20), fulfilling Psalm 118:22 and Isaiah 28:16. He is the rejected stone who becomes the foundation of a renewed spiritual house – one that is new, yet remains firmly connected to Israel's story. In him, the structure is joined together and grows into "a holy temple in the Lord" (Eph. 2:21). The *ekklesia* is not an abstract philosophical or theological construct. It is a temple made of living stones, bound together by the Spirit, and marked by the presence of a God who reconciles Jew and any other ethnic group in Christ.

Acts 15 and the Terms of Inclusion

The Jerusalem Council recorded in Acts 15 represents a watershed moment in the unfolding of God's redemptive plan. As Gentiles begin to respond to a thoroughly Hebraic gospel in growing numbers, a pressing theological question emerges: must Gentile believers be circumcised and observe the law of Moses to be saved? The council of the elders of the *ekklesia* in Jerusalem was convened to address this very concern. While we, in our 21st-century context, tend to take the meaning of that word "saved" very individualistically, you must remember that the early Church always thought in terms of the covenant community. For them, salvation was inseparable from belonging to the covenant community.

This conviction led some Jewish believers – especially those from a Pharisaic background – to insist that Gentiles could only be saved and included in the covenant community by adopting Jewish identity through circumcision and *Torah* observance (Acts 15:1,5). In their view, non-Jewish followers of Messiah need to renounce their own ethnic backgrounds and cultures to truly belong. But Peter gets up and reminds the assembly that God had already poured out the Holy Spirit on Gentiles, just as he had on Jewish believers at Pentecost, "making no distinction between us and them" (Acts 15:9). This divine initiative challenged all attempts to require anything beyond faith – beyond believing loyalty – in Jesus for full inclusion.

James, the brother of Jesus and leader of the Jerusalem church, delivers the decisive verdict. Quoting Amos 9:11-12, he proclaims that "the tent of David" is being rebuilt, so that "the remnant of mankind may seek the Lord, and all the Gentiles who are called by my name" (Acts 15:16-17). Significantly, James does not interpret Gentile inclusion as the end of Israel's story, but as its fulfillment. The coming in of the nations is not evidence for Israel's replacement, but for Israel's restoration. God is enlarging Israel's tent – not tearing it down.

The council's decision is both theological and pastoral. Gentiles are welcomed into the people of God without the requirement of circumcision or full *Torah* observance. Instead, they are expected to follow four specific guidelines: abstain from things polluted by idols, from sexual immorality (*porneia*), from meat of strangled animals, and from blood (Acts 15:20,29).

These guidelines echo the laws for foreigners (resident aliens) living in Israel found in Leviticus 17-18, where they were expected to avoid idolatry, improper use of blood, and sexual immorality (Lev. 17:8,10,12; 18:26). These are not ceremonial laws for covenant membership, but ethical boundaries so that Jews and non-Jews can have table fellowship with one another. Some scholars compare these rules to the later Noahide laws of rabbinic Judaism – basic moral standards for non-Jews living among Jews. Although the full Noahide framework developed later, evidence shows that early Jewish communities already expected Gentile God-fearers living and worshiping among them to follow certain ethical norms.[91]

So, the four rules in Acts 15 do not function as a new law, but as a missional accommodation: a way for Jewish and Gentile believers to live together in community without unnecessary offense. Gentile believers are not required to become Jews but are encouraged to respect Israel's standards of holiness when sharing community life. The Jerusalem Council's wisdom is in embracing Gentiles without demanding assimilation – affirming both unity and diversity within the Body of Messiah.

As restorationists, we view Acts 15 not just as a pivotal event in history, but as a blueprint for today's church life. The post-Acts 15 *ekklesia* – deeply rooted in Second Temple Judaism yet open to the nations – reflects the ideal form of Messiah's Body. While later movements – Lutheran, Reformed, Anabaptist, or Pentecostal – reclaimed important truths, none fully recovered the dynamic, Spirit-filled fellowship of Jews and Gentiles described in Acts. Many churches, especially those shaped by Reformation traditions, retained hierarchical structures from Roman Catholicism rather than returning to the relational and participatory ethos of the early *ekklesia*. By affirming Gentile inclusion without coercion, Acts 15 offers a model for the "one new man": a covenant family where Jews and Gentiles worship the same Lord while honoring their unique callings within God's grand design.

---

91 Craig S. Keener, *Acts: An Exegetical Commentary,* vol. 3, 2260-2269. Keener cautions against a direct equation of the apostolic decree in Acts with the later Noahide code, but affirms there is clear continuity of ethical expectations, with the former "foreshadowing" or paralleling the latter in significant ways.

Olive Tree Theology (Rom. 11:17-24)

Paul's olive tree metaphor in Romans 11:17-24 powerfully illustrates Gentile inclusion and Israel's ongoing role in God's redemptive plan. Opposing both replacement theology and dual-covenant separatism, Paul affirms that there is only one covenant people: God remains faithful to his promises to Israel's patriarchs.

Gentile believers are not a new tree growing alongside Israel's olive tree; they are wild branches grafted into its cultivated root, sharing the same nourishing sap of Israel's story (Rom. 11:17-18). This image stresses both unity and dependence – Gentiles draw their life from the same patriarchal root, not from their own origin or merit. Paul's point is clear: Gentiles were once "strangers to the covenants of promise" (Eph. 2:12), yet by God's mercy have been "brought near by the blood of Christ" (v.13). Their place is not earned or deserved but granted purely by grace.

Paul also insists that the natural branches – ethnic Israelites – are not rejected or discarded. Some were broken off because of unbelief, not ethnicity. Gentile believers are explicitly warned: "Do not become proud, but fear.… It is not you who support the root, but the root that supports you" (Rom. 11:18,20). Arrogance and presumption, Paul warns, lead the Church away from humility, making it prone to antisemitism and theological error. Ignorance of Israel's continuing role has often fueled such attitudes throughout history.[92]

Gentile believers in the Jewish Messiah have not replaced Israel. Instead, they are shown mercy alongside the Jewish remnant. The story is ongoing: Paul expects that those Jews who turn from unbelief will be grafted in again. This re-grafting is both natural

---

92   See Rom. 11:25. Paul uses the Greek word *agnoein* (ἀγνοεῖν), "to be unaware," which often prefaces serious theological error (cf. 1 Cor. 12:1; 1 Thess. 4:13).

and anticipated (Rom. 11:23-24).[93] God's promises to Israel are irrevocable (v.29) and broken-off branches are not discarded but await restoration.

This forms the heart of "Olive Tree Theology:" the *ekklesia* remains rooted in Israel's covenant. Gentile inclusion never comes at Israel's expense. The Church is not a new tree, but the renewed and expanding tree of Israel, pruned and regrafted through Messiah. Paul's metaphor is deliberately striking. Grafting wild branches into a cultivated tree was rare. Typically, the reverse happened. Paul uses this reversal to highlight the surprising mercy of God and the expansion of his people: Gentiles are brought in not to replace Israel but to provoke them to faith and to demonstrate God's unfailing mercy (Rom. 11:11, 31). A biblically grounded "Olive Tree Theology" rejects the final rejection of the Jewish people.

Ultimately, restorationist theology calls the Church to remember its roots: to see itself as grafted into the story of covenant and faithfulness that began with Abraham and will be fulfilled in the restoration of all Israel: "And in this way all Israel will be saved" (Rom. 11:26).[94]

Distinction Without Division

The unity of the *ekklesia* embraces the distinct identities of Jews, Gentiles, and all nations within it. Scripture consistently portrays unity as harmonious diversity rather than uniformity. This is why Paul describes the *ekklesia* as the "Body of Christ": just as a body has many members with different functions, so God's people include Jews and Gentiles, each with unique callings and covenantal roles

---

93   David H. Stern, *Jewish New Testament Commentary*, rev. ed. (Clarksville, MD: Lederer Books, 2023), note on Rom. 11:23-24, pp. 383-386.

94   Jeremiah 11:16; Hosea 14:6; cf. Ps. 52:8.

(Rom. 12:4-8; 1 Cor. 12:12-27). True biblical unity honors and celebrates diversity of identity, calling, and gifting.

Paul affirms that Gentile believers are full participants in the Body of Messiah, sharing one salvation, one Spirit, and one Lord with Jewish believers in him (Eph. 4:4-6). This inclusion, however, upholds Israel's unique calling and honors broader ethnic distinctions. Through the "Body of Christ" metaphor (1 Cor. 12), Paul celebrates not only spiritual gifts but also the rich ethnic and covenantal diversity within the *ekklesia*. Just as a body thrives through its many unique members, so the *ekklesia* flourishes when Jews and Gentiles – each with their own identity, history, and calling – are united in Messiah. As James D. G. Dunn observes, "Paul's vision of the body of Christ is of a unity which consists in diversity, that is, a unity which is not denied by diversity, but which would be denied by uniformity, a unity which depends on its diversity functioning as such – in a word, the unity of a body, the body of Christ."[95] Diversity is not a threat to unity but its essential foundation.

The principle of distinction without division is embodied in the sacraments of baptism and communion. In baptism, believers are united with Messiah and joined to his one Body: "For in one Spirit we were all baptized into one Body – Jews or Greeks, slaves or free – and all were made to drink of one Spirit" (1 Cor. 12:13). The focus here is not on uniformity, but on shared participation in a common spiritual reality. Baptism draws believers together while honoring their diverse heritages.

Similarly, communion – also known as the Lord's Supper – is more than a ritual remembrance. It is a shared recognition of the Body of Messiah. Paul urges the Corinthians to "discern the body"

---

95   James D. G. Dunn, *The Theology of Paul the Apostle* (Grand Rapids: Eerdmans, 1998), 564.

rightly (1 Cor. 11:29), referring both to Jesus' crucified body and to the community of believers composed of Jews and Gentiles. Failing to honor the diversity within that Body – through partiality or contempt – brings judgment (1 Cor. 11:27-30). To recognize the Body is to honor the distinct identities and gifts of all members of Messiah's people across every ethnic line.

This vision of one new man is richly textured, not colorless or cultureless. The nations retain their distinct identities when they come to Messiah, each bringing their unique glory into the New Jerusalem (Rev. 21:24). Likewise, Israel does not vanish into the nations but continues to fulfill a distinct covenantal role. Paul consistently upholds this differentiation. For example, he declares that the gospel is God's power for salvation "to the Jew first and also to the Greek" (Rom. 1:16) and refers to "my kinsmen according to the flesh… to whom belong the adoption, the glory, the covenants…" (Rom. 9:3-4). The present tense of these affirmations shows that Israel's calling is not a relic of the past, but an enduring reality.

Within the restored *ekklesia*, there is neither hierarchy nor uniformity between Jew and Gentile. Instead, mutual honor replaces rivalry and jealousy. Paul's words – "the eye cannot say to the hand, 'I have no need of you'" (1 Cor. 12:21) – apply not only to individuals and their spiritual gifts, but also to entire ethnic groups within Messiah's Body. Gentile believers need the Jewish people, both historically and in the present, just as the Jewish remnant needs Gentile believers, through whom Israel will be stirred to jealousy and renewal (Rom. 11:11).

Restorationist theology celebrates this vision of differentiated unity. The "one new man" is not a homogenized people, but a reconciled community, diverse yet deeply united, not only with God but with one another. This covenant family embraces its variety, joined not through cultural assimilation but through shared allegiance to Messiah. Rooted in faith, expressed in baptism and communion, and sustained by mutual honor, this kind of unity stands as a prophetic witness to the world, a glimpse of the age to come.

Unity as Eschatological Witness (John 17; Eph. 4)

Jesus' prayer in John 17 offers a profound glimpse into the heart of Messiah before his crucifixion. At its core is his deep desire for unity among his followers: "that they may all be one, just as you, Father, are in me, and I in you... so that the world may believe that you have sent me" (John 17:21). This is not a call for superficial agreement or institutional conformity, but for a spiritual oneness rooted in shared life with the Father and the Son, a unity that mirrors the communion of the Trinity and powerfully testifies to the truth of the gospel.[96]

Paul expands this vision in his epistles, especially Ephesians 4, where unity is portrayed not just as a relational aspiration but as an eschatological sign. "There is one body and one Spirit... one Lord, one faith, one baptism" (Eph. 4:4-5). These are not mere theological preferences, but foundational realities defining God's renewed people. Unity is not simply the end goal of the mission; it stands as a living testimony that Messiah has truly come.[97]

Paul also outlines the path toward this unity: the fivefold ministry. Christ gives apostles, prophets, evangelists, shepherds, and teachers "to equip the saints for the work of ministry, for building up the body of Christ, until we all attain to the unity of the faith" (Eph. 4:11-13). This equipping leads to corporate maturity and alignment

---

96 John 17:21 emphasizes the missional dimension of unity: "so that the world may believe." Jesus' own credibility before the world is linked to the visible oneness of his followers.

97 Paul's use of "one body, one Spirit, one Lord" in Ephesians 4:4-6 echoes the Shema (Deut. 6:4), grounding new covenant unity in Israel's foundational confession of faith.

with God's redemptive purposes. The aim is not uniformity, but a richly diverse Body working together under the headship of Jesus.

I cannot emphasize enough that this unity does not erase distinction. The same chapter that proclaims "one body" also affirms that "grace was given to each one of us according to the measure of Christ's gift" (Eph. 4:7). The Body is composed of different parts, each with unique functions, but all working together under one Head. This echoes Paul's earlier metaphors in Romans 12 and 1 Corinthians 12, where he affirms both diversity and interdependence within the Body of Messiah.[98] True unity honors the distinct callings of both Israel and the nations, of Jew and Gentile, without flattening their identities.

As discussed in the previous section, the sacraments of baptism and communion already testify to this unity. In baptism, believers are immersed into "one body" by "one Spirit" (1 Cor. 12:13). In the Lord's Supper, the Corinthian church is exhorted to "discern the body" (1 Cor. 11:29), which is a call to recognize and honor the gathered, diverse community of believers in Messiah.[99]

Restorationist theology sees this unity not only as a theological necessity but as an eschatological witness. The reconciled Body of Messiah – Jews and Gentiles, distinct yet united – is a foretaste of the age to come. It looks forward to the day when the nations will worship together in Jerusalem (Isa. 2:2-4) and when every tribe and tongue will join in declaring the glory of the Lamb (Rev. 7:9-10).[100]

---

98   See Rom. 12:4-8 and 1 Cor. 12:12-27. Paul insists that no part of the Body can say to another, "I have no need of you."

99   On 1 Cor. 11:29, see Gordon D. Fee, *The First Epistle to the Corinthians* – New International Commentary on the New Testament (Grand Rapids, MI: Eerdmans, 1987), pp. 563-564. Fee argues that "discerning the body" refers not only to Christ's body but also to the gathered community as in 10:17 (see also pp. 469-470).

100   The eschatological vision of unity in Isa. 2:2-4 and Rev. 7:9-10 is foundational to restorationist theology, which sees the reconciled *ekklesia* as a prophetic preview of the restored Kingdom.

The unity of the *ekklesia* is a prophetic signpost. It points forward, revealing what God is doing now and what he will ultimately complete when Messiah returns.

Pastoral Reflection: Living the Mystery

The mystery revealed in Ephesians 2-3 is not simply a theological concept to ponder. It is meant to shape the Church's very identity and witness to the world. If Jews and Gentiles are called to be one new man in Messiah, this reality should transform how we live, worship, and relate to one another as members of the *ekklesia*.

Paul embodied this mystery in his ministry. He willingly suffered so Gentiles could be included (Eph. 3:1,13), seeing this not as leaving Israel behind, but as bringing the nations into Israel's hope through Messiah. For Paul, the restoration of Israel and the reconciliation of the nations form one story moving toward fulfillment. The unity of Jew and Gentile is central to the gospel and crucial for the Church's mission.

When our congregations are shaped by this vision, we learn to value not only multiethnic diversity but also the unique covenantal identities of Jew and non-Jew and the interdependence among all ethnicities within the Body. True unity comes not from erasing our differences, but from honoring each other's distinct callings in Messiah. This kind of community requires humility, patience, and a fresh appreciation for God's faithfulness to his promises. As Paul urges, "welcome one another as Christ has welcomed you, for the glory of God" (Rom. 15:7).

Unity must also be lived out at the table. As we saw in the previous section, baptism and communion are not only personal rituals. They are covenantal demonstrations. We were "all baptized into one body" (1 Cor. 12:13), and in partaking of the one bread, we "who are many are one body" (1 Cor. 10:17). These are visible affirmations of our restored fellowship in Messiah, Jew and Gentile, slave and free, male and female, without erasing the uniqueness of each member.

Finally, this unity is missional. Jesus prayed, "that they may become perfectly one, so that the world may know that you sent me" (John 17:23). The oneness of Jew and Gentile in Messiah is a prophetic sign to the world that Jesus is indeed the Son sent by the Father. Our disunity hinders our witness. Our reconciliation declares his Lordship.

The path ahead will not be easy. The global Church has inherited centuries of misunderstanding, division, and even outright antisemitism. But we are not without hope. The olive tree still stands. The wall of hostility has already been broken by Jesus' death on the cross. And the Spirit is still at work forming a people in whom and through whom the mystery of Jew and Gentile unity is being demonstrated.

May we renew our commitment to being this "one new man" – a holy temple where each distinct stone is built together as a dwelling place for God (Eph. 2:22). Let us reject both uniformity and division and embrace the challenging yet beautiful path of unity in diversity. May our lives bear witness to God's wisdom, now revealed through the *ekklesia* even to the rulers and authorities in the heavenly places (Eph. 3:10).

"This mystery is that through the gospel the Gentiles are heirs together with Israel, members together of one body, and sharers together in the promise in Christ Jesus. ... [God's] intent was that now, through the church, the manifold wisdom of God should be made known to the rulers and authorities in the heavenly realms, according to his eternal purpose that he accomplished in Christ Jesus our Lord."
(Ephesians 3:6, 10-11 NIV)

Chapter 9

Torah, Identity, and the New Covenant People

The restoration promised in the prophets is not merely a return to land, temple, or sovereignty. It is a renewal of the heart. Central to the New Covenant is the transformation of human beings from within. The prophets Jeremiah and Ezekiel envisioned a day when *Torah* would be written on hearts of flesh, instead of on tablets of stone. "I will put my law within them," God declares through Jeremiah, "and I will write it on their hearts. And I will be their God, and they shall be my people" (Jer. 31:33).

This promise is echoed in Ezekiel's vision of national renewal proclaimed just before the famous valley of dry bones. The prophet declares, "I will give you a new heart, and a new spirit I will put within you... and cause you to walk in my statutes and be careful to obey my rules" (Ezek. 36:26-27). In this context, the "new heart" marks a radical inner transformation: God replaces a heart of stone with one of flesh, creating in his people an awakened desire for truth and an authentic capacity for obedience. This renewal is not achieved through external ritual or human effort. Rather, it is the miracle of divine grace by which the Spirit internalizes *Torah* and restores a living covenant relationship between YHWH and his people. Thus, the prophets envision restoration as more than an outward return or a national revival. It is the Spirit-empowered fulfillment of God's intent for his people to reflect his law from the inside out, moving from merely outward obedience to genuine covenantal faithfulness.

The earliest Jewish followers of Jesus did not perceive the New Covenant as abolishing *Torah*, but as realizing its deepest intentions in and through Messiah. They understood that God had not given his Spirit to annul his commandments but rather to enable genuine, Spirit-empowered obedience from the inside out. In this view, the work of the Spirit fulfills what *Torah* pointed toward: life shaped not by external compulsion but by internal transformation and covenant loyalty. Paul captures this vision when he writes that "the righteous requirement of the law might be fulfilled in us, who walk not according to the flesh but according to the Spirit" (Rom. 8:4), expressing that the New Covenant empowers believers to embody what God has always desired: a people who keep his instruction through renewed hearts, not in response to external pressure.

This inward renewal does not dissolve the outward distinctions God has established. When *Torah* is inscribed on the hearts of believers, it does not erase ethnic identity or cultural heritage. Instead, it creates a foundation for genuine unity in Messiah that celebrates covenantal diversity rather than flattening it. Far from enforcing uniformity, the Spirit's work enables Jews and Gentiles to remain distinct yet reconciled and united within one Body, each maintaining their God-given calling even as they are joined together in one family. Thus, because the Spirit writes *Torah* on the heart, believers can honor their unique identities while sharing true unity in Messiah.

To understand this properly, we must return to the Hebrew concept of *qahal* – the assembly of God's covenant people. The *qahal* of Israel, which first gathered at Sinai (Deut. 9:10), was the prototype for the renewed assembly formed in Acts 2. The Greek word *ekklesia*, often translated as "church," is the term used in the Septuagint to translate *qahal*. Thus, the first-century Jewish disciples did not view themselves as forming a new religion, but as the restored and Spirit-filled *qahal* – the covenant people of Israel reconstituted around the risen Messiah.

This reconstitution includes both continuity and expansion. It begins with the faithful Jewish remnant and extends to the Gentile nations, just as the prophets foresaw (Isa. 2:2-3; Zech. 8:23). The *ekklesia* is not a departure from Israel's story, but its continuation and fulfillment in Messiah. The *Torah* is far from obsolete and now finds its fulfillment in a people whose hearts are circumcised by the Spirit.

As we explore in the sections ahead, these restored people are called to walk a careful path. Their unique identities and callings must be respected without turning them into idols. The pursuit of unity is essential, but it must not come at the cost of the diversity God has given. *Torah* is not a means to earn righteousness. Rather, it stands as a witness to God's faithfulness – his ongoing work to renew his people and fulfill his promises.

Jewish and Gentile Believers: One Messiah, Distinct Callings

The gospel does not erase differences. It redeems them. From the very beginning, God's plan of redemption embraced both Israel and the nations. With the arrival of Jesus, the promises given to the patriarchs were not revoked but confirmed (Rom. 15:8). The nations are welcomed – not to become Jewish, but to join the already-existing covenant people as fellow heirs, sharing in the promise found in Messiah Jesus (Eph. 3:6). The New Covenant, therefore, brings unity without demanding uniformity. In Messiah, Jews and Gentiles are united, yet each continues to walk a path shaped by their unique calling.

The "one new man" in Ephesians 2 refers to a reconciled community – Israel renewed in Messiah and enlarged to welcome the Gentiles.[101] This new reality is not a homogenized identity in which covenantal distinctions vanish. Instead, Paul's vision is of a culturally diverse, Spirit-filled *qahal*: an assembly of Jews and Gentiles who each maintain their distinctive roles within God's unified family, rather than a generic blend in which all differences are erased. In Messiah, unity is forged not by losing what makes each community and ethnicity unique, but by bringing those differences together in shared faith and purpose.

This vision is rooted in the Hebrew Scriptures. From the calling of Abraham, God's intent was to bless "all the families of the earth" through his offspring (Gen. 12:3). Israel was set apart as a holy nation and priestly people (Ex. 19:5-6), called to embody God's purposes among the nations. The inclusion of the Gentiles does not mean that Israel's calling has been cancelled. Instead, it has been amplified. As Isaiah foresaw, Israel would be "a light to the nations" so that salvation might reach "to the end of the earth" (Isa. 49:6).

This distinctiveness continues in the New Covenant. Paul affirms it when he says, "Was anyone at the time of his call already circumcised? Let him not seek to remove the marks of circumcision. … Let each person lead the life that the Lord has assigned to him, and to which God has called him" (1 Cor. 7:18-20). This is not simply practical advice. It is theological wisdom. Jewish believers remain Jewish and don't become Gentiles. They have been called to live faithfully within the covenantal framework given to Israel. Gentile believers are not required to become Jewish but are still warmly welcomed into the people of God by faith, sealed with the

---

101 For a contemporary scholarly treatment of Jew-Gentile distinction within the "one new man," see Stuart Dauermann, "An Inconvenient Truth: A Right Understanding of the One New Man," *Interfaithfulness*, March 9, 2021, https://interfaithfulness.org/an-inconvenient-truth-a-right-understanding-of-the-one-new-man/, accessed on August 26, 2025.

Spirit, and called to walk in obedience to Jesus. One Messiah, but distinct callings.

This distinction is not a sign of division, but of divine design. Just as a body has many parts with different functions (Rom. 12:4-6), the one people of God consists of Jews and Gentiles who together form a holy dwelling for God. Their unity does not erase their distinctions, nor does the Spirit's work flatten their identities. It sanctifies them. The goal is not uniformity, but harmony in diversity under the Lordship of Messiah.

When Gentiles are grafted into the cultivated olive tree (Rom. 11:17-24), they do not become part of a new or generic religion. Instead, they are joined to the historic *qahal* of Israel – a people now reconstituted around Messiah Jesus. Gentiles share in the nourishment that springs from the Jewish root as redeemed participants who have been welcomed into the unfolding story of God's covenant. This is what makes the *ekklesia* both ancient and new: Israel's story continues, now opened wide to include the nations, united in the same promises and sustained by the same gracious root.

The mistake of much of Christian history has been to confuse unity with uniformity. This confusion has led, at times, to assimilationist pressures on Jewish believers to abandon their identity. At other times, it has led to triumphalist assumptions among Gentiles who assume they are now the new center of God's purposes and plans.[102] Both need to be rejected. Instead, we must rediscover the original vision of the apostolic *ekklesia*: one Shepherd, one flock (John 10:16), and within that flock a mosaic of identities that are called into covenant faithfulness. Jesus would lay down his life for his

---

102 A thorough discussion is offered in R. Kendall Soulen, *The God of Israel and Christian Theology* (Minneapolis: Fortress, 1996). He critiques supersessionism as the Church's core theological error and proposes a retrieval of Israel's ongoing role in salvation history.

Jewish sheep (v.15), but he would also bring in "other sheep that are not of this fold": the Gentiles who would listen to his voice (v.16).[103]

The "restoration of all things" (Acts 3:21) will not mean the loss of Israel's distinctiveness, nor the erasure of Gentile diversity. It will mean the fulfillment of both. The same Lord who is forming his one Body is also orchestrating the harmony of different callings, so that the whole people of God might reflect his multifaceted wisdom and glory to the world (Eph. 3:10).

The Ekklesia as Restored Humanity

The New Covenant people of God are more than a collection of individuals saved from judgment. They are a renewed humanity, restored in Messiah and formed into the *ekklesia* – the called-out assembly that reflects God's original design for creation. Paul captures this vision in Ephesians 2 when he declares that Messiah "has broken down in his flesh the dividing wall of hostility" (Eph. 2:14) and has created "one new man" (v.15). This is not merely a metaphor for spiritual peace but a reconstitution of Israel's *qahal*, the sacred assembly that first stood before God at Mount Sinai.

The *qahal*, God's gathered people, is not erased in the New Covenant. It is re-formed around the risen Messiah. In the Septuagint, *ekklesia* is the Greek word used for Israel's assembly, translating the Hebrew word *qahal*.[104] The early Jewish believers in Messiah, steeped in the Scriptures, would not have seen the *ekklesia* as a novel invention but as the prophetic continuation of God's

---

103 Some other commentators see the "other sheep that are not of this fold" as Samaritans. An example is messianic scholar Eli Lizorkin-Eyzenberg, *The Jewish Gospel of John: Discovering Jesus, King of All Israel* (self-published, 2019), 151-152.

104 The Septuagint consistently translates the Hebrew *qahal* (assembly) as *ekklesia*. See Deut. 9:10 (LXX), where the people gathered at Sinai are called the *ekklesia kuriou*, the assembly of the Lord.

covenant people, renewed by the Spirit and extended to include the nations.

This Spirit-filled *ekklesia* anticipates the new creation. In Ephesians 2:10, Paul speaks of believers as "created in Christ Jesus for good works, which God prepared beforehand." The language is Edenic: humanity is restored to its vocation, walking with God in faithfulness and fruitfulness. The community of believers becomes an outpost of God's reign, a foretaste of the restored world that is coming.

United with Messiah and raised with him (Eph. 2:6), the *ekklesia* shares in the life of the age to come. Its communal life, shaped by reconciliation and self-giving love, bears witness to God's cosmic restoration. Paul envisions the *ekklesia* not as a collection of people who each have their private faith but as a new creation community, joined together, growing into a holy temple, and indwelt by the Holy Spirit (Eph. 2:21-22).[105] This identity is sacred and must be nurtured. Just as Adam was entrusted with guarding Eden, preserving the sacred space God created (Gen. 2:15), so the *ekklesia* is called to guard the unity given by the Spirit (Eph. 4:3). When believers walk in humility, mutual honor, and covenantal love, they embody the unity that Jesus prayed for and that the world longs to see. The unity of the church is a gift to be guarded rather than a goal to achieve.

Identity and the Pitfalls of Assimilation

The restorative work of God in Messiah both values difference and creates deep unity. In this one new man, Jewish and Gentile believers are joined in covenant, not by losing their distinct callings, but by living them out together in harmony with God's purpose. The New Covenant forms a people whose shared allegiance to Israel's

---

105　See 1 Pet. 2:5 and Ezek. 37:27 for the concept of a Spirit-indwelt temple formed by a sanctified people.

Messiah unites them, not through uniformity, but by embracing diversity within one Body.

Jewish followers of Jesus are uniquely positioned to live out the continuity of God's covenant with Israel. Their identity and practices are not relics of a past age, but signs of God's enduring faithfulness and the prophetic hope of Israel's future. Far from being sidelined, the Messianic Jewish remnant stands at the center of the unfolding restoration story. The faithfulness of Messianic Jewish believers bears witness to the irrevocable calling given to the patriarchs (Rom. 11:29) and to the deeply Jewish roots of the *ekklesia* (Acts 1:6-8; Rom. 11:5).

At the same time, Gentile believers are fully welcomed into the covenant family through faith in Jesus. They are not called to adopt Jewish identity, but to follow the God of Israel with Spirit-empowered obedience rooted in their own heritage. The Jerusalem Council made this clear by setting out straightforward, unifying terms for Gentile inclusion within the Body of Messiah (Acts 15:1-29). The apostles affirmed that Jews and Gentiles are saved on equal terms through Jesus, and that each is encouraged to maintain their God-given identity. This equality allows and expects Jewish believers to continue in Jewish covenantal life, and Gentile believers to retain their unique identity as Gentiles within God's people.

Restoration affirms identity. Jewish believers remain Jews. Gentile believers remain Gentiles. Both are nourished by the same root, indwelt by the same Spirit, and welcomed into the same household of God. The *ekklesia* truly thrives as its members faithfully live out their unique callings, treating one another with mutual honor and joy. When Paul urges believers to "discern the body" (1 Cor. 11:29), he is inviting them to appreciate the beauty and diversity within God's people, especially in the shared experience of the Lord's Supper.

The unity found in Messiah takes its inspiration from Eden – a place where diversity flourished in God's presence. In the garden, distinctions were blessings, not barriers: male and female, humanity and earth, night and day – all woven together in a sacred design. In the renewed community, this pattern of harmony-in-diversity is restored. We point to a God who heals and reconciles, and we celebrate - not erase – the beauty of our differences. He is inviting his people to become who they were always meant to be, together in Messiah.

Renouncing Distortion

The vision of the "one new man" in Messiah is too precious to be misunderstood or minimized. Yet throughout church history, this foundational truth has often been distorted, leading to two opposite errors that must be carefully rejected if we are to walk in the gospel's unity and live out the Kingdom's promises.

First, the "one new Gentile" distortion is found in supersessionist theology. This view holds that the Church has replaced Israel and that Jewish identity no longer matters in God's redemptive plan While well-intentioned in its desire for unity, this view, which developed as early as the second century in some Church Fathers (e.g., Justin Martyr, Irenaeus), undermines the integrity of Scripture and erases the enduring covenant God made with the Jewish people.[106] It forgets that Gentile believers are grafted into Israel's tree, not the other way around, and that Paul still speaks of Israel's irrevocable calling.[107]

---

106 For early expressions of supersessionist theology, see Justin Martyr, *Dialogue with Trypho* (c. 155-160 CE), especially chapters 11 and 123; and Irenaeus, *Against Heresies*, Book IV. These writings already suggest that the Church, not Israel, is now the true people of God.

107 See Rom. 11:17-24 and Eph. 2:11-22 for Paul's extended metaphor and teaching on Gentile inclusion.

Second, some expressions of the "One Law" movement promote what we might call the "one new Jew" distortion. This view argues that all believers – both Jews and Gentiles – are required to keep the same *Torah* practices, from circumcision and kosher laws to the full observance of the Mosaic law. Although often motivated by a sincere love for God's commandments, it ignores the distinct callings of Jews and Gentiles. It also overlooks the decision of Acts 15, where the apostles welcomed Gentiles without requiring them to become Jews.[108]

Good theology avoids both extremes. Replacing Israel or forcing everyone to become Jewish harms the Body of Messiah. Instead, God calls us into a unity that values our differences. It is a covenant partnership where Jews and Gentiles keep their callings but walk together in Jesus.[109] This is how we show the world the beauty of the one new man: restored, united, and radiating the truth of God's ongoing covenant faithfulness.

Pastoral Reflection: Living as a Distinct Yet United People

The story of restoration is not just theological but deeply pastoral. At its heart lies a question every follower of Jesus must ask: What does it mean to belong to the covenant people of God today? For Jewish believers in Messiah, the call is to remain faithful to the identity God has given to them, without shame, without compromise, and without pressure to blend into a Gentile Christian mold. Holding to Jewish practice, culture, and rhythm is not legalism when done in faith and devotion. It flows out of covenant loyalty. The world does not need fewer Jews who follow Jesus. It needs more.

---

108 Cf. Acts 15:19-21.

109 See 1 Cor. 7:17-20, where Paul counsels Jewish and Gentile believers to remain in their respective callings, and Gal. 2:7-9, where the apostles affirm differentiated missions while extending the right hand of fellowship, expressing covenantal partnership in Messiah.

For Gentile believers, the invitation is just as profound: not to become Jewish, but to be grafted in with humility, reverence, and joy. This means rejecting both supersessionism and imitation. Gentiles are not second-class members of God's family, but neither are they called to erase the rich distinctions that give texture and meaning to covenant life. Instead, they are invited to honor the root, learn Israel's story, and share in the promises – all while embracing the beauty of their own God-given identity.

Unity in Messiah is not uniformity. The Church is not defined by bland sameness, but as a beautiful mosaic of diverse callings knit together in one Body. Just as the tribes of Israel camped around the tabernacle and as the members of a body each have unique functions, the *ekklesia* is created for harmony in difference. Our unity is found not in flattening identity but in exalting Jesus together, each offering distinct gifts for the good of all.

Let us reclaim the wisdom of Acts 15. The apostles and elders did not insist on uniformity but instead discerned a Spirit-led way of inclusion, honoring both Israel's calling and the welcome extended to Gentiles. This remains the model for the Body of Messiah today. We are called to resist pressures toward conformity – whether urging Jewish believers to assimilate or Gentiles to become Jews. Rather, let each walk faithfully in their own calling, anchored in Messiah and bound together in covenant love. This is the beauty of the one new man: a community both united and diverse, rooted and expanding, distinct yet inseparable – a foretaste of the age to come.

"…walk in a manner worthy of the calling
to which you have been called,
with all humility and gentleness, with patience,
bearing with one another in love,
eager to maintain the unity of the Spirit
in the bond of peace.
There is one body and one Spirit—
just as you were called to the one hope
that belongs to your call—
one Lord, one faith, one baptism,
one God and Father of all,
who is over all and through all and in all."

(Ephesians 4:1-6)

Chapter 10

The Wound in the Body: Christian Antisemitism and the Drift from Israel

The earliest days of the *ekklesia* were marked by extraordinary unity across deep cultural divides. Jewish and Gentile believers were joined together in Messiah, forming a Spirit-filled community rooted in Israel's Scriptures and hope. Yet this unity was hard-won, and the price of maintaining it grew higher over time.

As the gospel spread beyond Judea into the wider Roman world, new tensions surfaced. Many in the Jewish community rejected Jesus as Messiah, resulting in growing alienation between Jewish followers of Jesus and their synagogues (John 9:22; Acts 13:45-46). At the same time, large numbers of Gentiles were drawn into the movement, stirred by the Spirit and the promise of restoration. Yet these newcomers often lacked familiarity with Israel's story and *Torah*, which began to challenge the identity of the early *ekklesia*. As the community grew more diverse, it became harder to maintain true unity.

These tensions were not just theological. They were also political and social. Under Roman rule, Jewish distinctiveness was often seen as suspicious or rebellious. Gentiles who associated with Jews or observed Jewish customs risked persecution and social exclusion, so many began to distance themselves from the Jewish roots of their faith. At the same time, Jewish followers of Jesus faced isolation, were rejected by their synagogues and viewed with mistrust by the increasingly Gentile Church.[110]

By the early second century, divisions within the *ekklesia* became increasingly evident. While the apostles had fiercely guarded the unity of Jew and Gentile in one Body (Eph. 2:14-16), later church leaders began to interpret Christianity through Gentile cultural lenses – often drawing on Hellenistic philosophy. Gradually, the biblical terms "assembly" (*ekklesia*) and *qahal* of Israel gave way to the language of "church" – reflecting a shift away from the community's original identity as a united, covenantal people. As this transformation deepened, the memory of a single Body anchored in Israel's restored remnant faded from view, resulting in a predominantly Gentile Church.

Writings from figures like Ignatius of Antioch (c. 110 CE) reflect this early drift. Though affirming Jesus as the Jewish Messiah, Ignatius urges believers to avoid "Judaizing," pushing for a separation rather than fighting for continuity.[111] His concerns were

---

110 See for a discussion on the "parting of the ways" Annette Yoshiko Reed, *Jewish-Christianity and the History of Judaism* (Tübingen: Mohr Siebeck, 2018), 15-22.

111 Ignatius, *Letter to the Magnesians*, 8:1; *Letter to the Philadelphians*, 6:1. Magnesians 8:1: "For if we are still living according to Judaism, then we confess that we have not received grace. ... It is monstrous to talk of Jesus Christ and to practice Judaism. For Christianity did not believe in Judaism, but Judaism in Christianity." Ignatius here cautions believers that adhering to Jewish customs/law as a basis for Christian identity is to fall away from the grace found in Christ. He uses the term "Judaize" explicitly and draws a sharp contrast—urging a distance from those who mix or continue "Jewish" observances. Philadelphians 6:1: "But if anyone interprets Judaism to you, do not listen to him; for it is better to hear Christianity from one who is circumcised than Judaism from one who is uncircumcised." Here, Ignatius distinguishes "Judaism" (as a way of life or religious system) from "Christianity," urging separation, and emphasizing not the continuity but the break. Ignatius' tone is not one of seeking creative continuity with the Jewish roots of the faith but rather urging clear separation and even viewing "Judaism" as an earlier stage superseded by Christ. Holmes and other translators note that these letters are some of the earliest explicit evidence for a rift and polemical boundary-drawing between Christians and Jews, or those who would continue in both. Ignatius is suspicious of any blurring of the boundaries. This is widely recognized as an early move away from continuity with the synagogue and the Jewish communal framework.

likely pastoral, aimed at protecting Gentile believers from legalism, but they inadvertently reinforced a growing divide.

What began as subtle distancing would, over time, harden into a theological parting of ways. The "one new man" vision of Ephesians 2 was gradually redefined, not as a reconciled people preserving both Jewish and Gentile identity under Messiah, but as a newly Gentile-centered Church in which Jewish particularity was absorbed or erased. The seeds of division had been sown.[112]

The Rise of Anti-Jewish Rhetoric

As the Jesus movement spread into the broader Greco-Roman world, the early *ekklesia* began to take on a distinctively Gentile character. While the gospel retained its Jewish roots in Scripture and practice, it increasingly encountered and adapted to the cultural assumptions of its new environment. In this transition, a troubling pattern emerged: the rise of anti-Jewish rhetoric within Christian theology.

Some of the earliest Church Fathers, such as Justin Martyr, Tertullian, and John Chrysostom, wrote passionately against Judaism. These writings often contained hostile characterizations of Jews as stubborn, blind, or even accursed. Jewish rejection of Jesus was interpreted not simply as a tragic decision, but as proof that God had abandoned his covenant with Israel. Around 160-170 CE, Melito of Sardis introduced the idea of deicide (the murder

---

112 See, for instance, Mark S. Kinzer, *Postmissionary Messianic Judaism: Redefining Christian Engagement with the Jewish People* (Grand Rapids, MI: Baker Academic, 2005), 232. Kinzer asserts, "... we presented a bilateral ecclesiology in solidarity with Israel. According to such an ecclesiology, the ekklesia requires a living connection to the Jewish people. In the first generation of the Yeshua movement, the ekklesia of the circumcision provided such a link. It was a visible, sociological reality. In the generations that followed, this ecclesiological bridge collapsed, and the two corporate entities – the church and the Jewish people – apparently went their own separate ways."

of God): the Jews had killed God by crucifying Jesus. This would poison Christian attitudes against the Jewish people for millennia.[113]

Even as the Church affirmed the Hebrew Scriptures, many early theologians began to reinterpret Israel's story in ways that severed it from its covenantal context. Especially after the destruction of Jerusalem in 135 CE, the hope of Israel's restoration appeared – humanly speaking – impossible to many. Drawing heavily on Greek philosophical frameworks, figures like Origen and Clement of Alexandria spiritualized the promises of Scripture: the land of Israel became an allegory for heaven, the temple a metaphor for the soul, and *Torah* obedience a shadow of higher spiritual truth. Their theology was shaped not only by Platonic ideals, but also by present realities: a devastated Jerusalem, a scattered Jewish people, and the apparent eclipse of national hopes. Facing a world where Israel's national hope seemed lost, these Church Fathers increasingly understood Scripture's fulfillment as spiritual and universal rather than physical and national.[114]

The development of their theology was deeply shaped by Platonism, which tended to devalue the physical in favor of the spiritual. Earthly practices like circumcision, food laws, and Sabbath observance were viewed as immature or inferior. The tangible, embodied aspects of Jewish covenant life – so central to the biblical narrative – were gradually replaced with universalized and abstract ideals. In this view, Israel's uniqueness was treated as an obstacle, rather than a gift to be cherished.

---

113 Melito of Sardis wrote: "God has been murdered, the king of Israel has been put to death by an Israelite right hand" (*On the Pascha*, 96).

114 An example is Justin Martyr, who writes in his *Dialogue with Trypho* (11.5): "the true spiritual Israel, and descendants of Judah, Jacob, Isaac, and Abraham... are we who have been led to God through this crucified Christ, as shall be demonstrated while we proceed" (c. 155 CE).

This led to a growing theological justification for the Church to distance itself from its Jewish foundations. Supersessionism – the idea that the Church replaced Israel as God's people – became not just a matter of political convenience but a core doctrinal assumption.[115] As Israel's story was spiritualized and its covenantal identity redefined or dismissed, the *ekklesia* increasingly saw itself as a wholly new people, severed from its Jewish roots. This shift distorted Christian identity and ultimately paved the way for centuries of antisemitism within the Church.

Tragically, these theological distortions reverberated far beyond Christianity. A telling example is Islam, which emerged in the seventh century. Early Christian Church Fathers and polemicists such as John of Damascus classified it as a Christian heresy or cult that explicitly denied foundational Christian doctrines such as the incarnation, the Trinity, Jesus' divinity, and his death and resurrection, while appropriating elements from both Jewish and Christian traditions. The theology of Islam constitutes the ultimate replacement theology: it claims not only to supersede Judaism, but also to correct, complete, and fulfill Christianity – presenting itself as the final revelation and the sole true religion of God. In doing so, Islam positions itself as the successor to both Israel and the Church – amplifying and radicalizing the supersessionist trajectory that had begun in post-apostolic Christianity.[116]

---

115 R. Kendall Soulen, *The God of Israel and Christian Theology*, 118, note 6. Soulen distinguishes three forms of supersessionism: economic, punitive, and structural. He asserts, "The first two designate explicit doctrinal perspectives, i.e., that carnal Israel's history is providentially ordered from the outset to be taken up into the spiritual church (economic supersessionism), and that God has rejected carnal Israel on account of its failure to join the church (punitive supersessionism). ... Structural supersessionism... renders the Hebrew Scriptures largely indecisive for shaping Christian convictions about how God's works as Consummator and as Redeemer engage humankind in universal and enduring ways."

116 See Joel Richardson, *When a Jew Rules the World* (Leawood, KS: Winepress Media, 2015), 162-167.

The idea that the *ekklesia* would supersede Israel was never the vision of the apostles. Paul pointedly warned Gentile believers in Rome not to become arrogant toward the Jewish people, reminding them: "It is not you who support the root, but the root that supports you" (Rom. 11:18). The root – God's covenant with Abraham and his promises to Israel – remains alive and indispensable. To sever the Body of Messiah from its Jewish foundation is to cut the Church off from its very source of life.

Institutionalization of the Divide

As the center of the *ekklesia* shifted away from Jerusalem toward Rome and Constantinople, the informal tensions between Jews and Gentiles became formalized in church structures and creeds. What began as a theological drift soon hardened into ecclesiastical policy. This stage marked a turning point, not just in church history, but in the Church's relationship to its own roots.

A major milestone was the Council of Nicaea in 325 CE, convened by Emperor Constantine. At Nicaea, crucial Christological affirmations were made (e.g., the deity of Jesus). The council also addressed the dating of Passover, replacing it with a universally observed Easter that would no longer be tied to the Jewish calendar. This was not merely a liturgical adjustment. Constantine's own words reveal the deeper motive: "It appeared an unworthy thing that in the celebration of this most holy feast we should follow the practice of the Jews... let us have nothing in common with the detestable Jewish crowd."[117] Such language signaled a deepening desire to define Christian identity in contrast to the Jewish people. This was a deliberate theological and political move to distance the Church from Israel's story.

---

117 Constantine, *Letter to the Churches Regarding Easter*, recorded in Eusebius, *Life of Constantine*, Book 3, Chapter 18.

In the decades that followed, this trajectory only intensified. The Council of Laodicea (circa 363-364 CE) explicitly forbade Christians from observing the Jewish Sabbath, celebrating Jewish festivals, or following Jewish dietary customs.[118] These rulings not only pressured Gentile believers to further sever ties with the Jewish roots of their faith and community but also directly targeted Jewish followers of Jesus who sought to remain faithful to their ancestral identity. What had once been honored as covenantal faithfulness – living in accordance with *Torah* – was now increasingly labeled as legalism, Judaizing, or even heresy.

Meanwhile, influential church historians and theologians such as Eusebius of Caesarea promoted a narrative in which the Church had inherited all the promises of Israel, while the Jews had inherited only the curses. Eusebius cast Constantine as a kind of new Moses, leading a newly purified people, now unhitched from Jewish tradition, into a spiritual Promised Land.[119]

What began as a family dispute eventually hardened into an institutional divorce. Christianity, once deeply rooted in Israel's story, broke away and allied itself with the Roman Empire – redefining its identity in deliberate opposition to the Jewish people. The movement that started as a branch of Judaism was gradually reshaped by Roman imperial power, and Jewish believers in Jesus found themselves increasingly isolated: unwelcome among Jews who did not accept Jesus as Messiah and marginalized within a

---

118 Canons 29 and 37 of the Council of Laodicea discuss the prohibition of Sabbath observance and participation in Jewish feasts.

119 See, for a survey of Constantine as a new Moses, Finn Damgaard, "Propaganda Against Propaganda: Revisiting Eusebius' Use of the Figure of Moses in the Life of Constantine," in *Eusebius of Caesarea: Tradition and Innovations*, ed. Aaron P. Johnson & Jeremy Schott (Washington, DC: Center for Hellenic Studies, 2013), 132-155, accessed on Nov. 23, 2025, https://chs.harvard.edu/chapter/6-propaganda-against-propaganda-revisiting-eusebius-use-of-the-figure-of-moses-in-the-life-of-constantine-finn-damgaard/.

Church that viewed Jewish identity as suspect or even subversive. Even today, this remains a deep wound in the Body of Messiah – a wound that has bled across centuries and continents. Instead of the shared table of Acts 15, the Church built dividing walls. Instead of honoring both Jew and Gentile, it adopted systems that systematically excluded Jewish followers of Jesus. This was neither the vision of Paul nor Jesus, but it became the path the Church chose for the next fifteen hundred years.

The One New Man Distorted

The language of "one new man" in Ephesians 2 originally described the Spirit-forged reconciliation and unity between Jew and Gentile in Messiah. Over time, however, this vision was gradually distorted. Instead of remaining a community that honored both Jewish and Gentile callings within one Body, the Church redefined the "one new man" to mean a distinctly Gentile-centered religion, one in which Israel's story, covenants, and Jewish identity were effectively dissolved or set aside.[120]

This distortion took many forms, as we saw earlier as well. One of the earliest – emerging in the late second century – was the "one new Gentile" paradigm. In this view, unity in Christ was redefined to mean that Jewish believers were expected to abandon their distinctive identity and practices. Circumcision, Sabbath-keeping, the feasts, and dietary laws were dismissed as outdated or even heretical. Jewish followers of Jesus faced increasing pressure to assimilate, becoming indistinguishable from their Gentile counterparts.[121] Over time, Gentile cultural norms became the

---

120 See Ephesians 2:14-16 for Paul's vision of Jew-Gentile reconciliation as "one new man."

121 The Epistle of Ignatus to the Magnesians 10:7-8 gives a clear example of how Jewish believers in Jesus were pressured to set aside their Jewish distinctiveness: "It is monstrous to talk of Jesus Christ and to practice Judaism. For Christianity did not

standard for Christian life, and Jewish expressions of faith were largely excluded or stigmatized.

As a result, the Church gradually cut itself off from its own story. Without the anchor of Israel's Scriptures, Messiah, and covenants, it lost sight of its origins and purpose. The model set at the Jerusalem Council, where the apostles upheld both unity and distinction, faded into obscurity. Paul's olive tree metaphor was neglected, and the Church increasingly reimagined itself not as grafted in, but as a new planting, disconnected from its Jewish roots. This created a "Church without roots," a Body estranged from the very soil that once nourished it. Supersessionist theology took hold: the Church was reimagined as the new Israel, wholly replacing the old. Jesus was stripped of his Jewish identity. Even the apostles came to be remembered not as Jewish witnesses to Israel's Messiah, but as ecclesiastical symbols or miracle-workers.

The consequences were enormous. When the "one new man" vision is stripped of its Jewish foundation, it is no longer a prophetic signpost to God's restoration of humanity. Instead, it becomes an assimilation project, a forced sameness that silences the voice of Jewish believers within the Body of Messiah. And when Jewish identity is erased, so too is the Church's ability to rightly understand its calling in the world.

A second distortion we highlighted before surfaced in recent decades within the Hebrew Roots and One Law movements. If we can characterize the first distortion as "one new Gentile," this may rightly be called "one new Jew." In reaction to centuries of supersessionism, these groups rightly affirm the value of *Torah* but

---

believe in Judaism, but Judaism in Christianity..." John Chrysostom (late 4th century) in his sermons *Against the Jews* rails against Jewish practices, denouncing Jewish Christians and urging them to abandon "Jewishness" in all its forms. Jewishness increasingly became incompatible with Christian identity and membership in the church.

go a step too far by insisting that all believers – Jew and Gentile alike – must keep all Mosaic commandments. This includes circumcision, kosher laws, the Sabbath, and biblical feasts. While often motivated by love for God's commandments and a desire to restore biblical roots, this approach erases the distinct callings of Jews and Gentiles, collapsing diversity into a single, uniform religious identity. It is a new legalism, a deviation from the apostolic teaching in Acts 15, which maintained distinct but united covenant paths for Jews and Gentiles.[122] The "one new Jew" distortion essentially mirrors the error of "one new Gentile:" it overlooks the wisdom of Acts 15, where the apostles, guided by the Spirit, welcomed Gentiles into God's family without requiring Jewish conformity.[123]

We must avoid both distortions – the "one new Gentile" and the "one new Jew." Instead, we are called to pursue the true unity envisioned in the "one new man:" unity in diversity, not mere uniformity. Ephesians 2 calls Jew and Gentile not to erase what makes them unique, but to become a reconciled family through the cross, where distinct identities are cherished within one sacred community. This is not a homogenized assembly, but a spiritual temple built of many different stones, joined together as a dwelling place for God.

Recovering this vision reconnects us to the wisdom of Acts 15, to Paul's teaching in Romans 11, and to Jesus' high priestly prayer in John 17. These are not relics of the past but living prophetic maps

---

122   See David Rudolph, *One New Man, Hebrew Roots, Replacement Theology: How to Restore the Jewish Roots of the Christian Faith Without Getting Weird* (Southlake, TX: The King's University, September 8, 2021), https://collective.tku.edu/wp-content/uploads/2021/09/One-New-Man-Hebrew-Roots-Replacement-Theology.pdf, 7-27, for a critique of 'One Law' approaches that require all believers to keep the same Mosaic commandments and the theological risks of erasing Jewish-Gentile distinction.

123   See Acts 15:28-29, where the apostles explicitly refrain from imposing the law on Gentile believers; also, Romans 14 and 1 Corinthians 9:20-21, where Paul affirms the legitimacy of diverse religious practice and identity within the Body of Messiah.

pointing us to the future. They call us back to the "one new man" as it was meant to be: restored, rooted, and radiant with the glory of God's covenant faithfulness.

Consequences Through History

The theological drift away from Israel never remained confined to ivory towers or dusty manuscripts. It spilled out into pulpits, church policies, and eventually fueled widespread persecution. Once the Church had redefined itself in opposition to the Jewish people, it opened the floodgates to centuries of anti-Jewish hostility, often cloaked in theological language and ecclesial authority. Throughout the medieval period, Jews across Europe were subjected to forced conversions, discriminatory laws, exclusion from public life, confinement to ghettos, expulsions, and systematic attempts to marginalize and dehumanize them – all justified by Christian doctrine and rhetoric. Church-sanctioned violence, including the Crusades and the Inquisition, brought suffering under the name of Christ. Pogroms – organized massacres – swept across Christian lands. Jewish people were frequently scapegoated during times of plague, famine, or political unrest.[124]

Even though the Protestant Reformation restored many core biblical truths, it still suffered from the same historic error regarding Israel. Martin Luther, the father of the Reformation, initially displayed a hopeful posture toward the Jewish people, believing they would respond positively to a gospel unburdened by Catholic corruption. But when his hopes were disappointed, his later writings became extremely harsh and hostile toward Jews, using bitter language and calling for actions that fueled centuries of Christian antisemitism, particularly within Protestant circles. This is an infamous quote from one of his later writings, *On the Jews and*

---

124 Joel Richardson, *When a Jew Rules the World*, 132.

Their Lies (1543): "What shall we Christians do with this rejected and condemned people, the Jews? ... First, to set fire to their synagogues or schools and to bury and cover with dirt whatever will not burn, so that no man will ever again see a stone or cinder of them. ... Second, I advise that their houses also be razed and destroyed. ... Third, I advise that all their prayer books and Talmudic writings, in which such idolatry, lies, cursing and blasphemy are taught, be taken from them."[125] The echoes from Luther's writings would resurface time and again, often in devastating ways.

On November 9, 1938, the night before Luther's birthday, Nazi Germany launched *Kristallnacht*, the "Night of Broken Glass," during which hundreds of synagogues were burned, thousands of Jewish businesses and homes were vandalized, and over 30,000 Jews were arrested. Contemporary estimates suggest several dozen to a few hundred Jews died during or shortly after *Kristallnacht*, though precise numbers remain disputed. Nazi ideologues intentionally timed the attacks so that the synagogues would be burning on Luther's birthday. Though Hitler himself was not a confessing Christian, he exploited centuries of Christian antisemitism, both Catholic and Protestant, to justify his genocidal agenda.[126] The silence of much of the German church and its historic theological biases against the Jewish people made it easier for such evil to thrive.

125　This is the original quote: "Was sollen wir Christen tun mit diesem verworfenen und verfluchten Volke, den Juden? ... Zuerst, wir stecken ihre Synagogen oder Schulen an, und verbrennen und überdecken mit Erden alles, was nicht brennet, damit niemand je einen Stein oder Asche davon sehe. ... Zweytens, ich rath, daß man auch ihre Häuser zerreisse und zerstöre. ... Drittheils, ich rath, daß man ihnen alle ihre Betbücher und Talmudschriften nehme, worin solche Götzendienste, Lügen, Flüche und Lästerungen gelehret werden."

126　See Richard Steigmann-Gall, *The Holy Reich: Nazi Conceptions of Christianity, 1919-1945* (Cambridge: Cambridge University Press, 2003), for an analysis of Hitler's complex relationship to Christianity and the Nazi exploitation of Christian antisemitism for ideological legitimation.

Even after the Holocaust, many parts of the Church have struggled to fully acknowledge the depth of their complicity. Supersessionist thinking – the belief that the Church has replaced Israel – remains deeply embedded and often goes unchallenged in seminaries and church traditions. As a result, antisemitism has resurfaced in new forms, in our day most visibly as anti-Zionism, which denies the Jewish people's right to live as a nation in their ancestral land.[127] While criticism of modern Israeli politics is legitimate, questioning Israel's very existence on theological grounds is something else: it usually springs from the same replacement theology – now clothed in new language like liberation theology or postcolonial theology – that has long fueled Christian antisemitism.

This trend is particularly visible in western churches that have become disconnected from the Jewish roots of the gospel and have never truly repented of replacement theology. Without a restored understanding of Romans 11, Ephesians 2, and the calling of Israel, the Church remains vulnerable to repeating the errors of the past. These errors cost millions of lives and dishonored the name of the Jewish Messiah.

Pastoral Reflection: A Call to Repentance and Restoration

The wound of Christian antisemitism is not merely historical. It is profoundly spiritual. It is a wound in the Body of Messiah – still open and in need of honest recognition, deep repentance, and active healing. The story of the Church's drift from Israel is not a distant or abstract legacy; it is our story. We have inherited both its pain and its responsibility. Now, we are called to face it and respond with courage and humility.

---

127 "Why Anti-Zionism Is a Form of Antisemitism," World Jewish Congress, accessed November 27, 2025, https://www.worldjewishcongress.org/en/anti-zionism.

Throughout this chapter, we have traced the painful journey: from subtle early tensions to theological betrayal; from ecclesial policies to political violence; and from distortion to denial. We have seen how the original vision of the "one new man" was distorted. And we have seen how that distortion led not only to estrangement from Israel, but also to a loss of the Church's own identity.

But the story does not have to end in despair. In Christ, there is always a path to restoration. The gospel does not call us back to nostalgia but invites us to repentance. This is where restoration begins. We repent of the ways the Church has despised the root that supports it (Rom. 11:18). We repent of theological systems that erased or replaced the Jewish people, of our silence in the face of hatred, and of misrepresenting the Jewish Messiah. We acknowledge the times we have neglected the vision of unity with distinction found in Ephesians 2 and Acts 15. We repent not just of sins of the past, but of the attitudes and actions that still repeat these same errors today.

Our repentance is not political. It is covenantal. It is not about endorsing every decision of the modern State of Israel. It is about affirming God's enduring covenant with the Jewish people. Romans 11:29 still stands: "The gifts and the calling of God are irrevocable."

A Church that forgets this lesson will always be vulnerable to the next theological trend that simply repackages the old error of supersessionism, making it more agreeable in appearance, but equally destructive in substance. Whether the threat comes wrapped in anti-Zionist rhetoric, syncretic theologies, or misguided calls for religious uniformity, the danger persists. The only antidote is a return to Scripture, to the heart of Messiah, and to the humility of branches graciously grafted in. We do not stand above Israel. We do not replace Israel. By God's mercy, we are joined with Israel in one covenant family, held together by the blood of Messiah.

So let the Church return. Let pastors and leaders teach the whole counsel of God, including the Hebrew Scriptures and the covenants made with Israel. Let congregations rediscover the richness of a gospel rooted in Abraham's story, fulfilled in Jesus, and extended to the ends of the earth. Let our discipleship, our worship, and our mission reflect the "one new man" as it was meant to be: restored, rooted, and radiant with covenant faithfulness. Let us take our place, not over Israel, but beside her. And in doing so, we join the story of restoration that God is writing in the here and now.

"So I ask, did they stumble in order that they might fall? By no means! Rather, through their trespass, salvation has come to the Gentiles, so as to make Israel jealous. Now if their trespass means riches for the world, and if their failure means riches for the Gentiles, how much more will their full inclusion mean! ... For if their rejection means the reconciliation of the world, what will their acceptance mean but life from the dead?... Do not be arrogant toward the branches."
(Romans 11:11-12, 15, 18)

Chapter 11

The Return of the King:
Jesus and the Restoration of Israel

As the risen Jesus stands on the Mount of Olives, ready to ascend into heaven, his disciples ask a question that went to the very heart of Israel's hope: "Lord, will you at this time restore the kingdom to Israel?" (Acts 1:6). These words are neither naïve nor misguided. The disciples weren't imagining a vague spiritual kingdom. They were longing for a concrete, covenantal restoration, echoing the promises spoken by the Hebrew prophets: the reunification of Israel's tribes, the defeat of her enemies, and Messiah's reign from Jerusalem over a renewed earth.[128]

Jesus' response has often been misunderstood as a rebuke: "It is not for you to know times or seasons that the Father has fixed by his own authority" (Acts 1:7). Note that he does not deny the hope in which their question is rooted. Instead, he redirects their attention to what is theirs to know and do, while reminding them that the timing of the Kingdom's restoration belongs to the Father alone. Meanwhile, he gives them their mission: "You will receive power when the Holy Spirit has come upon you, and you will be my witnesses... to the end of the earth" (Acts 1:8). Jesus doesn't dismiss their Kingdom hopes; rather, he frames their commission within the very story they so earnestly awaited. The Kingdom's message

---

128 See Isa. 2:1-4; Ezek. 37:15-28; Amos 9:11-15. Jewish expectations of national restoration were grounded in prophetic promises of land, peace, justice, and divine rule centered in Zion.

is going global, yet it is still Israel's Kingdom – and Israel's Messiah who will reign at its center.

This continuity is confirmed as Acts unfolds. Soon after, Peter proclaims that Jesus must remain in heaven "until the time for restoring all the things about which God spoke by the mouth of his holy prophets long ago" (Acts 3:21). The restoration spoken of by prophets like Isaiah, Jeremiah, and Ezekiel always included the renewal of Israel and the nations streaming to Zion – the fulfillment of God's promises centered in his covenant people.[129]

Jesus' ascension didn't end Israel's story. It launched the next chapter. The disciples weren't sent away from Jerusalem, but out of it. Filled with the Holy Spirit, they were sent to invite both Jews and Gentiles into the promise of restoration through the Jewish Messiah. The hope they held on to – that God would restore the Kingdom to Israel – wasn't cut short. Yet it wouldn't happen on their timeline but on God's.

Israel's Partial Hardening and Future Salvation

Paul's words in Romans 11 are both sobering and hopeful. He cautions Gentile believers in Rome: "Lest you be wise in your own sight, I do not want you to be unaware of this mystery" (Rom. 11:25). This mystery is not a forever-hidden secret, but a divine plan now brought to light through the gospel. For the present, Paul explains, there is a partial hardening – a temporary resistance to Messiah within Israel – "until the fullness of the Gentiles has come in." This signals a stage in salvation history where God's grace reaches the nations, paving the way for Israel's future restoration.

---

129 Peter's reference to God restoring "all the things" (Acts 3:21) links Messiah's return to the fulfillment of the prophetic promises to Israel and the nations. This "restoration of all things" includes Israel's national renewal.

Yet even now, God's covenant promises to Israel stand unbroken. The partial hardening is neither total nor permanent. Jewish believers in Paul's time – and today's growing Messianic Jewish movement – demonstrate the ongoing faithfulness of God. The inclusion of Gentiles does not bring Israel's story to an end. Rather, it moves it toward fulfillment, as the nations' ingathering ultimately serves the restoration that the prophets foretold.

Paul warns Gentile believers in Rome against two spiritual pitfalls, as we saw earlier: arrogance (Rom. 11:18) and ignorance (v.25) regarding God's purposes for Israel. Arrogance leads to a sense of superiority and spiritual pride, while ignorance results in a failure to grasp the unfolding story of God's covenant faithfulness. Paul makes clear that the combination of these attitudes fosters a distorted theology – one in which the Church imagines itself as a replacement for Israel, rather than a people graciously grafted into Israel's promises. Against this, Paul boldly affirms: "all Israel will be saved" (v.26). This is not necessarily a promise that every individual Jew will believe but a prophetic assurance of national restoration, a collective turning back to God, as foretold by the prophets.[130]

Paul quotes Isaiah: "The Deliverer will come from Zion; he will banish ungodliness from Jacob" (Rom. 11:26; cf. Isa. 59:20). This points to a future salvation that is both spiritual and national, grounded in God's unshakable covenant faithfulness. Paul's use of Isaiah here is not incidental. Rather, it places Israel's restoration and renewal at the very heart of his gospel. For Paul, Isaiah's vision of redemption is woven into God's larger plan of salvation for both Israel and the nations, fulfilling promises that reveal the depth of God's enduring commitment to his people.

---

130   See, for an extensive discussion, David H. Stern, *Jewish New Testament Commentary* on Romans 11:26a, pp. 387-392.

Paul continues with a bold affirmation: "For the gifts and the calling of God are irrevocable" (Rom. 11:29). These words echo through history as a direct challenge to the claims of supersessionism. God has not revoked his covenant with Israel. Her story is not finished. It is still unfolding, with faithfulness and sorrow, mystery and hope. Messianic Jewish scholar David H. Stern explains that the "gifts" and "calling" refer to the privileges, covenants, and divine election granted to the Jewish people. These are not conditional, nor can they be transferred to another group. Paul's use of the word "irrevocable" is a deliberate rejection of any theology that claims God has abandoned Israel. According to Stern, this verse stands as one of the clearest scriptural rebukes to replacement theology. It affirms that Israel remains central to God's redemptive plan – not just in the past, but in the present and future.[131]

Paul calls Gentile believers to humility, reminding them that their inclusion in God's people is an act of mercy, not the result of merit. They have been grafted into a tree they did not plant and welcomed into a covenant to which they were not the original heirs. Their purpose is not to replace Israel, but to stir her to a holy longing – a "jealousy" (Rom. 11:11) not rooted in rivalry but awakened by the witness of Gentiles who walk in the fullness of the Kingdom with gratitude and reverence for the God of Israel, and love for the Jewish people. True comprehension of this mystery should evoke deep humility in all followers of the Jewish Messiah, especially those from the nations. If God's faithfulness endures toward Israel, it ensures hope for everyone who is drawn into his story, reminding us that the unfolding narrative of redemption leads to the restoration of all things.

---

131 See David H. Stern, *Jewish New Testament Commentary*, on Romans 11:28-29, pp. 392-393.

The Time of Jacob's Trouble

Jesus' return is not an isolated event but the climactic moment in God's unfolding story – a story marked by profound suffering and promise. While eschatological frameworks differ within the global Church – amillennial, postmillennial, and premillennial alike – the prophetic testimony converges on this point: Israel's restoration and Messiah's return are bound together in God's redemptive plan

Before Israel welcomes her Messiah with the words, *Baruch haba b'shem Adonai*,[132] she must pass through a period of unparalleled anguish, foretold by the prophets as "the time of Jacob's trouble" (Jer. 30:7), a unique distress for Israel that precedes her restoration.[133] This turning point will emerge not in an age of peace but amid global upheaval, as "all the nations of the earth will gather against Jerusalem" (Zech. 12:3). In this hour, deep darkness gives way to redemptive dawn: "they will look on Me, on him whom they have pierced" (Zech. 12:10). Israel will recognize and embrace her Messiah – the One she once rejected.

This tribulation, described by Jesus as "a time of great distress, such as has not been from the beginning of the world until now, no, and never will be" (Matt. 24:21), presupposes Israel restored to her land and the nations mobilized against her.[134] The spiritual roots of this hostility – seen in ancient and modern manifestations of antisemitism – are ultimately enmity against YHWH, his Anointed, and Zion – the place where Messiah will reign (Ps. 2). While criticism

---

132 *Baruch haba b'shem Adonai* is the Hebrew behind "Blessed is he who comes in the name of the Lord" (Matt. 23:39), quoting Ps. 118:26. In Jewish tradition, this phrase often points to the coming of Messiah and is central to eschatological expectation. See Psalm 118:26; Matt. 23:39.

133 Jeremiah 30:7 identifies this period as "the time of Jacob's trouble," framing it as unique suffering before restoration.

134 Zechariah 12:3 envisions the nations gathered against Jerusalem, alongside Jer. 30:7-8 and Matt. 24:21 in describing an unprecedented eschatological crisis for Israel that presupposes her restoration to the land.

of Israel's politics may be valid, Psalm 2 warns that opposition to God's redemptive purpose for Zion is a recurring satanic pattern – one that manifests in various forms throughout history and is especially prominent in certain modern ideologies and movements directed against Jerusalem and God's covenant people, in particular in Islam.

A Tested Allegiance

In these last days, not all who profess allegiance to Jesus will bear the same cost. Those who distance themselves from Israel, ignoring the mystery of the olive tree, may avoid the world's fury. But those choosing covenantal solidarity with the Jewish people – God's firstborn (Exod. 4:22) – will share their reproach, for the same powers of darkness that rage against Zion also target her defenders. True allegiance will be tested, not by creeds, but by costly identification with those at the center of God's purposes.

When Jesus returns and judges the nations, the dividing line will be their treatment of "the least of these my brothers" (Matt. 25:40) – a phrase many scholars interpret first and foremost as referring to Jesus' Jewish kinsmen.[135] The nations will be judged according to how they respond to the Jewish people in their hour of crisis.

---

135 Although Matthew 25:40 can have a broader application (i.e., showing mercy to the marginalized), the literary and historical context shows that the primary and immediate referent of "my brothers" is Jesus' own people, the Jews. Joel Richardson, *When a Jew Rules the World*, 237-238, makes a compelling case for this view. Well-known Bible teacher Derek Prince had a similar understanding of this verse. Derek Prince states: "All nations are going to be judged by the way that they treat and relate to the brothers of Jesus. And remember, Jesus is a Jew and the Jewish people, even in their rejection by God and their disobedience, are still the brothers of Jesus. So, the dividing point between the nations, the sheep who are accepted, the goats that are rejected, will be the way they have dealt with Jesus' brothers, with Abraham and his descendants. Those who bless them will be blessed, and those who curse them will be cursed." See Derek Prince, "Aligning Ourselves with Israel," podcast audio, Derek Prince Ministries, accessed on September 20, 2025, https://www.derekprince.com/radio/145.

What is coming is not merely geopolitical. It is a time of spiritual trial preceding a new birth. The Great Tribulation is the labor pangs before Israel, in her darkest hour, cries, "*Baruch haba b'shem Adonai*" – triggering the return of the King of Glory not to Rome, not to Mecca, not to Washington DC, but to Jerusalem, the city of the Great King (Ps. 48:2; Matt. 5:35).

A Spirit of Grace and Supplication

Zechariah's vision points to the climactic moment when national repentance and spiritual renewal will break forth in Jerusalem: "I will pour out... a spirit of grace and pleas for mercy, so that, when they look on me... they shall mourn for him, as one mourns for an only child" (Zech. 12:10). This mourning will come as Israel reaches the darkest hour of its history – the "time of Jacob's trouble" – when, surrounded by hostile nations and with every other option exhausted, she turns to the Lord alone. Out of this pressure will rise the cry, "*Baruch haba b'shem Adonai*" (Matt. 23:39; Ps. 118:26). Jesus presents this cry of recognition and repentance as a condition for his return.

At that moment of surrender, the Spirit will be poured out. This outpouring is both personal and profoundly national, fulfilling ancient covenant promises (Jer. 31:31-34; Ezek. 36:26-27, 37:9-10). Israel awakens to her Messiah as the New Covenant reaches its climactic fulfillment, not just in scattered remnants but in the national rebirth Isaiah foresaw: "Can a nation be born in a day?" (Isa.66:8). The answer unfolds as the remnant becomes a people, the people become a nation, and that nation comes to life by the breath of restoration.

At the Heart of the Gospel Story

The restoration of Israel is not a side theme in Scripture. It is woven into the very fabric of the gospel of the Kingdom. From God's promise to Abraham that "in you all the families of the earth shall be blessed" (Gen.12:3) to the prophetic hope of Israel's renewal, the biblical storyline moves steadily toward the reconciliation of Israel and the nations under the reign of Messiah.

The promise of Genesis 12:3 is central to God's unfolding plan of redemption for both Israel and the nations. This blessing motif runs through the Old Testament, shaping the prophets' vision of Israel's restoration and pointing forward to the day when Jew and Gentile will be reconciled in Messiah's Kingdom. The Abrahamic covenant, which consists of land, descendants, and blessing for all peoples, provides the framework for God's redemptive mission. Again and again, the prophets echo this pattern: Israel is chosen, disciplined, and ultimately restored so that blessing may flow to all nations, culminating in the reign of Messiah.

Paul makes this clear in Romans 11: the salvation of the nations and the future salvation of Israel belong to a single divine plan. In Romans 9-11 Paul is wrestling with God's covenant faithfulness to both Israel and the nations. He asserts that Israel's present "partial hardening" is not evidence of God abandoning his covenant but part of a larger redemptive purpose. The "mystery" of Romans 11:25-32 is that Israel's temporary rejection opens the way for the fullness of the Gentiles to come in, after which "all Israel will be saved."

In this vision, salvation history is an integrated restoration process in which the reconciliation of Jew and Gentile is essential to understand God's promise-keeping character. For Paul, God's action in Messiah has opened covenant membership to all humanity, Jew and Gentile alike, without canceling his ancient promises to Israel. Rather than replacing Israel, the nations are grafted into Israel's own covenantal life, anticipating the day when the natural branches will be restored to their own olive tree (Rom. 11:24). From a restorationist perspective, this means the ingathering of the nations and the renewal of Israel are divinely ordered to occur in sequence – each serving the other in God's timing. The ultimate "restoration" is thus a twofold event: the ingathering of the nations and the final renewal of Israel. These are not competing destinies but inseparable parts of "one single divine plan" flowing from God's faithfulness to his covenant with Abraham and culminating in the gospel's fulfillment at Messiah's return.[136] So, according to Paul, Gentile inclusion is not the conclusion of God's work with Israel but a stage in its unfolding. The "fullness" of the nations coming in is directly linked to Israel's awakening, which Paul vividly describes as "life from the dead" (Rom. 11:15).

Peter echoes the same theme in Acts 3, urging his Jewish hearers to repent "that times of refreshing may come from the presence of the Lord, and that he may send the Christ appointed for you, Jesus" (Acts 3:19-20). He then declares that Jesus must remain in heaven "until the time for restoring all things" (Acts 3:21). In the flow of Peter's sermon, this "restoration" is rooted in "what God spoke by the mouth of his holy prophets long ago" (Acts 3:21b), recalling promises of Israel's renewal, covenant faithfulness, and restoration of the Kingdom of Israel under Messiah's reign (cf. Isa. 2:1-4; Jer. 31:31-34; Ezek. 36-37). The phrase "restoring all things" does not dissolve Israel's national hope into abstraction, but places Israel's restoration at the center of the larger renewal of creation. For Peter, just as for Paul, the restoration of Israel is not peripheral. It is central to the fulfillment of God's redemptive purposes, inseparably bound

---

136 Many interpreters read Romans 9-11 through a supersessionist lens, concluding that the Church has permanently replaced Israel in God's redemptive purposes. Such readings tend to view "all Israel" in Romans 11:26 as referring to the Church composed of Jew and Gentile together, rather than to ethnic Israel's future turning to Messiah. The text in Romans, however, shows that Paul upholds Israel's continuing role in God's covenant plan. This opens the way for a restorationist reading in which the salvation of the nations and the renewal of Israel are intertwined stages of the same eschatological hope.

up with the reconciliation of the nations and the ultimate renewal of all creation.[137]

The Church's mission unfolds within the same story that began with Israel. To neglect Israel is to diminish the scope of the gospel and to forget where the mission is heading: toward the day when Jew and Gentile are restored together under Messiah's reign.

Pastoral Reflection: Learning to Love Israel Again

The relationship between the Church and Israel is, in significant part, a story of estrangement. For centuries, walls of misunderstanding, prejudice, and at times open hostility have been erected – often in the very name of the One who came to break them down. Supersessionism, in both overt and subtle forms, has fueled Gentile pride and deepened Israel's wounding as God's covenant people. The tragic consequences of this posture are evident not only in theology books and pulpits but also in some of history's darkest episodes. Paul's warning in Romans 11 remains urgent: "Do not be arrogant toward the branches... remember it is not you who support the root, but the root that supports you" (Rom. 11:18).

Now is the time for humility. As the global Body of Messiah, we are summoned to lay aside pride and presumption, returning instead to the posture of gratitude that befits those grafted in by grace. The Jewish people are not a relic of the past nor a mere backdrop for someone else's end-times drama. They remain "beloved for the sake of their forefathers" (Rom. 11:28) and serve as

---

137 Many scholars recognize that "the restoration of all things" (Acts 3:21) is an schatological expression drawn from the prophetic hope of Israel's renewal (cf. Mal. 4:5-6 LXX; Isa. 49:6; 65:17-25). The Greek term *apokatastasis* was commonly used in the LXX to denote the reestablishment of Israel's covenantal order (e.g., Jer. 16:15; 24:6), and Luke's narrative consistently frames it in this way (cf. Acts 1:6; 15:15-18). Thus, the "restoration" in view is not merely a cosmic repair in the abstract, but the fulfillment of God's promises to Israel as the first stage in the renewal of the world, in keeping with the Abrahamic covenant that envisions blessing for "all the families of the earth" through Israel's restoration (Gen. 12:3; Gal. 3:8).

ongoing witnesses to the faithfulness of God. Covenant solidarity with Israel does not mean idolizing her but rather honoring the God who keeps his promises and aligning ourselves with his unfolding plan of redemption.

Such solidarity with Israel and the Jewish people is not abstract. It takes shape in prayer for the peace of Jerusalem, in standing against antisemitism in all its forms, in welcoming Jewish believers into full fellowship without forcing them to abandon their God-given identity, and in proclaiming the good news of Messiah with love and respect to both Jew and Gentile. It means rejecting both the "one new Gentile" of supersessionism and the "one new Jew" of distorted One Law theology and instead embracing the one new man Paul describes – Jew and Gentile reconciled to God and to one another in Messiah (Eph. 2:14-16).

The restoration of all things will come in God's appointed time, but the call to repentance and restoration is for now. May we be found as those who prepare the way for the Lord – humble, watchful, and longing for the day when Israel's veil is lifted, the nations rejoice, and the King returns to Zion. Until that day, let us take our stand together, rooted in the covenants, united in the Spirit, and advancing the gospel of the Kingdom to the ends of the earth.

"Behold, the Lord has proclaimed
to the end of the earth:
Say to the daughter of Zion,
"Behold, your salvation comes;
behold, his reward is with him,
and his recompense before him.
And they shall be called The Holy People,
The Redeemed of the Lord."
(Isaiah 62:11-12)

Chapter 12

The Millennium and Messiah's Reign from Zion

The vision of God's universal kingship is not merely an ancient prophecy. It is an essential part of the living prayer tradition of the Jewish people. Across the world – in Orthodox, Conservative, and Reform synagogues alike – every service concludes with the *Aleinu* prayer,[138] which ends by proclaiming the words of Zechariah 14:9: "The Lord will be king over all the earth; on that day the Lord will be one and his name one." This closing line ("the Lord will be one and his name one") echoes the opening confession of the *Shema* in Deuteronomy 6:4: "*Shema Yisra'el, Adonai Eloheinu, Adonai Echad*" ("Hear, O Israel: The LORD our God, the LORD is one"). In this way, Jewish liturgy binds together Israel's covenant confession and eschatological hope – the one God worshiped at Sinai will, in days to come, be universally acclaimed.

In the *Shema*, Israel remembers the covenant at Sinai, where YHWH revealed himself as the one true God and gave his *Torah* to form a priestly nation.[139] In *Aleinu*, Israel looks forward to Zion's

---

138 On the liturgical use of *Aleinu* and its quotation of Zech. 14:9 in synagogue worship, see Seth Winberg, "Aleinu," *My Jewish Learning*, accessed on August 6, 2025, https://www.myjewishlearning.com/article/aleinu/.

139 Throughout the biblical and post-biblical tradition, the Sinai narrative provides the foundation for Israel's ongoing role as a "priestly kingdom and holy nation" (cf. Exod. 19:5-6), recalling and reaffirming the covenant relationship each time the Shema is recited. This serves as more than a memory of the past. It functions liturgically and theologically to shape Israel's mission and self-understanding. The Shema ("Hear, O Israel: The LORD our God, the LORD is one") is not only a declaration of God's unique oneness, but also a covenantal pledge – committing Israel to love and obey the God who called them at Sinai and gave them the *Torah* to help shape their

future, when that same covenant God will be acknowledged by all nations. Every recitation of *Aleinu* weaves together the memory of God's revelation at Sinai, the Jews' ongoing covenant commitment, and their hope for the day when all humanity will acknowledge YHWH as King.

This hope is the horizon of the Messianic Age described by the prophets and in Revelation 20: a time when Israel is restored, the nations stream to Mount Zion in Jerusalem, and Messiah reigns in righteousness over the whole earth. It is the age in which the prayer of *Aleinu* will be answered in full, and the confession of the *Shema* will be the worship of every tongue.

Revelation 20 and the Earthly Reign of Messiah

The final book of Scripture closes with a sequence of visions that bridge the present age and the new creation. Faithful commentators differ in their interpretations, but in this book we proceed from a historic premillennial perspective that places Messiah's visible reign on earth after his return.

In Revelation 20:1-6, John sees an era in which Satan is bound, the righteous are raised from the dead, and Messiah reigns before the last rebellion and the final judgment. John repeats the phrase "a thousand years" six times, signaling a defined messianic era. The precise number is less important than the reality it describes: a distinct period in which the risen Messiah governs the earth from Jerusalem, fulfilling the hopes of Israel's prophets.[140]

Throughout church history, Christians have understood this "Millennium" in different ways.[141] Amillennialism doesn't take the

---

covenantal life and mission among the nations.

140 See for a discussion David H. Stern, *Jewish New Testament Commentary*, notes on Rev. 20:2-7, pp. 782-784.

141 For a summary of millennial views, see Renald Showers, "A Description and Early

"Millennium" as a literal time period, but understands it to be the present church age, with Satan's "binding" representing his defeat at the cross. Postmillennialism envisions the Millennium as an extended golden age within history, brought about by the advance of the gospel and the discipling of the nations, after which Christ will return to consummate his reign.

Preterism sees much of Revelation fulfilled in the first century, especially in 70 CE with the destruction of the temple in Jerusalem.[142] Full preterism claims all prophecy – including the resurrection and final judgment – has already been fulfilled and therefore leaves no future return of Christ. This falls outside historic Christian orthodoxy. Partial preterism holds that many prophecies were fulfilled in the first century, yet still expects a future visible return of Jesus, the resurrection of the dead, and final judgment.

Historic premillennialism, which is the view embraced in this book, teaches that Messiah will return after a period of tribulation to inaugurate a literal messianic era, reigning from Jerusalem in fulfillment of Old Testament promises to Israel and the nations. It holds to a post-tribulational rapture – that is, believers are gathered in the sky to welcome Christ at his coming, after the tribulation. This approach is called "historic" because it closely reflects the eschatological views of the earliest Church Fathers (such as Papias, Irenaeus, and Justin Martyr), who, following patterns from Second Temple Judaism, anticipated a visible Kingdom of God on earth after

---

History of Millennial Views," *Israel My Glory* (June/July 1986), accessed on Nov. 24, 2025, https://israelmyglory.org/article/a-description-and-early-history-of-millennial-views/.

142 An extensive survey of full and partial preterism and how they do not line up with Christian orthodoxy can be found in Reinhardt Stander, *Preterism, Futurism or Historicism? A Theological Analysis of Three Interpretive Schools of Apocalyptic Prophecy within the Doctrine of the Last Things* (PhD diss., Stellenbosch University, 2021), esp. pp. 64-66, https://scholar.sun.ac.za/server/api/core/bitstreams/d24074e1-fbcb-457a-9703-6b27afaf01b2/content (accessed on 24 Nov. 2025).

Messiah's arrival and the resurrection of the saints. Historically, this view was called chiliasm.[143]

Dispensational premillennialism also holds that Christ will return before a literal thousand-year reign. In contrast to historic premillennialism, it treats Israel and the Church as two distinct peoples in God's plan and teaches a pretribulation rapture, meaning the Church is taken to heaven before a seven-year tribulation. This system originated in the 1830s with John Nelson Darby, an Anglican minister and leader among the Plymouth Brethren in Britain, who systematized a new approach to biblical prophecy, dividing history into distinct "dispensations." This view spread rapidly in the United States, especially through the publication of the Scofield Reference Bible (1909), and further gained influence in evangelical circles via Bible institutes and popular literature, such as Hal Lindsey's *The Late Great Planet Earth* (1970), and the *Left Behind* series of Tim LaHaye & Jerry B. Jenkins (1995-2007) and their film adaptations.[144]

The strength of historic premillennialism is that it harmonizes Revelation 20 with the wider prophetic witness. Isaiah foresaw a time when the nations would live in peace under Messiah's rule (Isa. 2:1-4; 11:1-9). Zechariah envisioned the LORD as King over all the earth (Zech. 14:9). Ezekiel spoke of a restored Israel dwelling securely in the land (Ezek. 36-37). These promises have yet to be fulfilled in history and find no complete realization in the present age of the Church.[145]

---

143 The term chiliasm is derived from the Greek word *chilias*, which means "thousand."

144 For a survey and a critique of dispensational premillennialism, see Ariel Blumenthal, *One New Man*, 259-270.

145 For OT background to the messianic reign, see Isa. 2:1-4; 11:1-9; Zech. 14:9-21; Ezek. 36-37. John's vision of the Millennium in Revelation 20 is best understood as the literal consummation of these unfulfilled OT promises: an era in which the Messianic King rules, Israel is restored, and the nations experience true peace and justice. Amillennial / postmillennial readings do not see a literal fulfilment of these promises.

The Messianic era serves as a bridge between this present evil age and the eternal state. It is the time when Messiah will vindicate God's covenant faithfulness to Israel, bring justice to the nations, and display the beauty of God's government on earth before the final renewal of all things. On that day, the prayer of *Aleinu* will no longer be a petition – it will become the reality of a world ruled by the King from Mount Zion.

The Great War and the Two Suppers: Joy and Judgment

Before the Messianic reign described in Revelation 20 can begin, Scripture portrays a climactic confrontation between Messiah and the gathered forces of rebellion. John sees heaven opened and the Rider on a white horse, the Faithful and True One, coming to judge and wage war in righteousness (Rev.19:11-16). His robe is dipped in blood, his name is the Word of God, and the armies of heaven follow him. This is the moment when the King takes the field to establish his reign.[146]

At the heart of this final battle is a stark contrast between two banquets, both happening on earth. The first is the marriage supper of the Lamb, announced in Revelation 19:6-9 and foreshadowed in Isaiah's prophecy: "On this mountain the LORD of hosts will make for all peoples a feast of rich food, a feast of well-aged wine" (Isa. 25:6). It is the covenant celebration of Messiah's union with his purified Bride – consisting of the redeemed from Israel and the nations – and the proclamation that death has been swallowed up forever (Isa. 25:7-8).

---

146 John draws on Old Testament themes of divine warrior and Davidic King (e.g., Isaiah 63:1-6), using them to present Jesus as Messiah who executes righteous judgment and inaugurates God's final Kingdom. This scene marks the turning point when the King visibly intervenes in history, overcoming rebellion and establishing the conditions necessary for the messianic reign described in Revelation 20.

The second banquet could not be more different. Immediately before the battle, an angel calls "all the birds that fly directly overhead, 'Come, gather for the great supper of God, to eat the flesh of kings... captains... mighty men... horses and their riders... all men, both free and slave, both small and great'" (Rev. 19:17-18). This gruesome invitation echoes Ezekiel's prophecy against Gog and Magog: "Assemble and come, gather from all around to the sacrificial feast... and you shall eat fat till you are filled, and drink blood till you are drunk" (Ezek. 39:17-20). One celebration is for the redeemed to share the joy of their King. The other is the grim feast where the enemies of the King themselves become the meal.

In both visions, the feasts are covenantal in nature: one displays covenant mercy, the other covenant justice. They mark the final and irrevocable separation of eternal destinies – those invited to the marriage supper enter the joy of the Lord, while those summoned to the great supper of God encounter the wrath of the Lamb. Only after this decisive war and the removal of all who oppose YHWH, can the nations come in peace to worship at Jerusalem. The *Sukkot* celebration prophesied in Zechariah 14:16-19 becomes possible precisely because the rebellion has been crushed and the King now reigns unopposed from Zion.

The Torah Shall Go Forth from Zion

When the Great War is over, there can be peace. If Revelation 20 shows us the reign of Messiah in broad strokes, Isaiah 2:2-4 and Micah 4:1-4 paint its everyday reality. In the latter days, these prophets declare, the mountain of the LORD's house will be established above the hills, and all nations will stream to it. They will say, "Come, let us go up to the mountain of the LORD... that he may teach us his ways and that we may walk in his paths." And then comes the key line: "For out of Zion shall go forth the Torah, and the word of the LORD from Jerusalem" (cf. Isa.2:3 and Micah 4:2).

This is not a return to the legalism Paul opposed, but the universal reception of Messiah's righteous instruction. Here, *Torah* means God's teaching and instruction, his covenantal wisdom for life, not merely a legal code.[147] In the Messianic Age, Messiah himself will be the Teacher, and his word will be the standard by which nations live, settle disputes, and experience peace. The result is a disarmament unlike anything the world has ever known: "They shall beat their swords into plowshares... neither shall they learn war anymore" (Isa. 2:4).

The prophets saw this as the fulfillment of God's purpose for Israel from the beginning. At Sinai, God gave his *Torah* to form Israel into a priestly nation (Exod. 19:5-6). By reciting the *Shema* daily, the ancient Israelites – and Jews to this day – are constantly reminded of that covenant truth: "The LORD is one."[148] The *Aleinu* prays for its universal fulfillment: "On that day the LORD will be one and his name one" (Zech. 14:9). In the Messianic Age, Zion becomes the global Sinai. What was once heard by one nation at Mount Sinai will one day be taught to all nations from Mount Zion in Jerusalem.

---

147 Even though Paul critiques legalism in his writings, he never rejected *Torah* as God's revelation or wisdom. Rather, he opposed its distortion into a boundary-maintaining system that reinforced ethnic exclusivity –what he calls "works of the law." This reading reflects key insights from the New Perspective on Paul, first introduced by E. P. Sanders, who argued that Second Temple Judaism operated according to "covenantal nomism," not legalism, and further developed by James D. G. Dunn, who contended that "works of the law" refers to ethnic identity markers such as circumcision, food laws, and calendar observance, not moral effort. For Paul, *Torah* remains a covenantal gift; what he rejects is its misuse as a basis for boasting or excluding the nations from God's people. See E. P. Sanders, *Paul and Palestinian Judaism* (Philadelphia: Fortress, 1977) and James D. G. Dunn, *The New Perspective on Paul*.

148 The *Shema* is not just about confirming monotheism. It is structured to remind Israel of the God who revealed himself at Sinai and the benefits and obligations that flow from that encounter. This daily act holds together Israel's historical identity, covenant responsibilities, and ongoing mission as rooted in the *Torah*.

Even at the first Sinai, the covenant community was ethnically inclusive. When Israel came out of Egypt, a "mixed multitude" (Heb.: *'erev rav*; Exod. 12:38) went up with them – non-Israelites who joined in God's redemption and stood at the mountain to hear his voice. This foreshadows the Messianic Age, when redeemed nations will stand alongside restored Israel to receive Messiah's teaching from Zion. In that day, Israel's priestly calling will come to its fullness, blessing all the families of the earth in accordance with the promise to Abraham.

Today, most nations still rebel against YHWH and resist his laws, preferring to define right and wrong for themselves. But in the age to come, they will be glad to seek God's instruction. From Zion, Messiah will teach. From Zion, justice will flow. From Zion, the knowledge of the LORD will cover the earth as the waters cover the sea.

Land, Justice, and the Covenantal Hope Fulfilled

The Messianic Age will not be an abstract spiritual state, but a tangible fulfillment of God's promises in the very land he swore to Abraham, Isaac, and Jacob. The covenant God made with Abram included a solemn oath: "To your offspring I give this land, from the river of Egypt to the great river, the river Euphrates" (Gen. 15:18). These boundaries, never fully realized in Israel's history, will be restored when Messiah will reign from Zion. Ezekiel envisioned Israel regathered from all the countries into their own land, cleansed from their uncleanness, given a new heart and Spirit, and dwelling securely under the shepherd-King from David's line (Ezek. 36:24-28; 37:24-28).

Justice and righteousness will characterize Messiah's government. As Psalm 72 declares, he will "judge your people with righteousness, and your poor with justice" (Ps. 72:2), defending the cause of the needy and crushing the oppressor. Isaiah foresaw a ruler who would "judge with righteousness the poor, and decide with equity for the meek of the earth" (Isa. 11:4). His reign will be marked by the perfect balance of mercy and truth, justice and peace, not by the political compromises of this age.

The land itself will flourish under his blessing. Amos prophesied, "The mountains shall drip sweet wine, and all the hills shall flow with it… they shall plant vineyards and drink their wine, and they shall make gardens and eat their fruit" (Amos 9:13-14). Covenantal restoration unfolds in vivid agricultural terms: prophetic visions depict the land itself rejoicing and flourishing under the benevolent reign of its rightful King, signaling both divine blessing and the renewal of creation in response to covenant faithfulness. Joel also vividly described that future day when "the mountains shall drip sweet wine, the hills shall flow with milk, and all the streambeds of Judah shall flow with water" (Joel 3:18), signaling abundance, renewal, and joy as a result of the reign of Messiah.

The vision of these prophets is deeply Edenic. The prophets portray the restored land as sacred space, where God's presence dwells with his people, echoing the garden-temple imagery of Genesis 2. In Eden, humanity's vocation was to tend and keep God's sanctuary garden. In the Messianic Age, Israel will again dwell in a land made holy by the presence of the LORD, and the nations will stream to it to share in its blessings. The story that began in a garden will near its climax in a garden-like land, before reaching its completion in the new heavens and the new earth.

The Nations Flow to Zion: Israel Leads Again in Worship

The prophets foresaw not only Israel's restoration but also the willing submission of the nations to Messiah's reign. Zechariah envisions a time when survivors from all nations "shall go up year after year to worship the King, the LORD of hosts, and to keep the Feast of Booths" (Zech. 14:16).[149] The Feast of Booths – *Sukkot* – is not only the final harvest festival in Israel's agricultural calendar. Eschatologically, it points to the ultimate harvest, the final ingathering of the Gentile nations into the worship of the God of Israel. Isaiah pictures these nations streaming to Jerusalem, bringing their wealth and glory into the city of the great King (Isa. 60:5-11). In the Messianic Age, Israel's priestly calling (Exod. 19:6) will be fully realized at last, as the restored nation leads the world in worship and instruction.

This will be a unity without uniformity. The nations will retain their distinct identities and cultures, yet all will acknowledge the same God, worship in the same city, and be governed by the same righteous standard. The kings of the earth will bring the glory and honor of their nations into Jerusalem, not as subjugated peoples, but as redeemed, joyful participants in God's Kingdom (Rev. 21:24-26). The nations preserve their unique identities and splendor, contributing them to the King in Jerusalem not as the spoils of war demanded by conquest but as the joyful tribute of redeemed peoples – voluntary acts of worship.

The pattern was set long ago. At the first Exodus, the *'erev rav* ("mixed multitude") went up with Israel from Egypt (Exod. 12:38), joining the covenant people of Israel and journeying toward the promised land with them. In the Messianic Age, this pattern will reach its fullest expression as redeemed peoples from every nation join restored Israel in covenant life under Messiah's reign. This will be the ultimate pilgrimage, a global ingathering to Zion.

---

149 Zech. 14:16-19 anticipates a worldwide pilgrimage to Jerusalem in the Messianic Age, where all peoples actively participate in worshiping Israel's God and share in the celebration of *Sukkot*. The Feast of Booths is chosen specifically because it is both a festival of joyful harvest and a reminder of God's provision, symbolizing the nations' inclusion in covenantal blessings.

The Feasts as a Prophetic Framework for Restoration

The biblical feast cycle itself prophetically anticipates this redemptive drama. Passover (*Pesach*) found its fulfillment in Messiah's first coming, as the Lamb of God secured redemption through His blood. *Shavuot* (Pentecost) was inaugurated in Acts 2 with the outpouring of the Spirit, when God's *Torah* was inscribed on the hearts of Messiah's firstfruits. In the Messianic Age, this New Covenant promise will reach its climax as that same Spirit-empowered instruction flows forth from Jerusalem, writing God's law on every heart and extending his wisdom to all nations. *Sukkot* (the Feast of Tabernacles) will culminate in the nations gathering physically in Zion, rejoicing together in the manifest presence of the King.[150]

Before the ultimate *Sukkot*, the King's arrival will be heralded by "the last trumpet" (1 Cor. 15:52; 1 Thess. 4:16), echoing the Feast of Trumpets (*Yom Teruah*) as the prophetic signal of Israel's regathering and the inauguration of Messiah's reign from Zion.[151] Thus, the Millennium becomes both the consummation of Israel's story and a foretaste of the new creation, when God's dwelling will be with humanity forever (Rev. 21:1-4).

---

150 The biblical feasts are not merely commemorative but forward-looking, each one prophetically pointing to a pivotal moment in God's redemptive timeline: Messiah's sacrifice (Passover), the giving of the Spirit (*Shavuot*), and the ultimate ingathering of the nations (*Sukkot*) in the age to come.

151 Paul's "last trumpet" language in 1 Corinthians 15 and 1 Thessalonians 4 is rooted in Jewish liturgical and prophetic traditions regarding *Yom Teruah*, where the *shofar* (ramshorn, also translated as "trumpet") blasts were understood as calls to repentance, prophetic announcements, and preparations for divine intervention. Rabbinic and Second Temple sources often viewed the feast as marking the resurrection of the dead, the regathering of Israel, and the dawning of the Messianic Age. Paul frames the return of Christ as the ultimate fulfillment of these patterns: Israel's ingathering, the resurrection of the righteous, and the commencement of Messiah's reign from Zion.

Pastoral Reflection: Longing for Messiah's Reign from Zion

The hope of the Millennium is not a curiosity for end-time charts and prophetic timelines, but a call to lift our eyes. The prophets foresaw a day when Messiah would reign from Zion, Israel would be restored, and the nations would learn war no more. This is not some escapist fantasy. It is the anchor of our expectation – the sure promise of the One who cannot lie.

We live now in the "already and not yet." The King has come, the Spirit has been poured out, and the firstfruits of Israel and the nations have turned to Israel's Messiah. Yet the fullness is still ahead. The *Aleinu* prayer still rises from synagogues around the world: "The LORD will be king over all the earth; on that day the LORD will be one and his name one." We who believe in Jesus know that day will dawn when he returns to sit on David's throne in Jerusalem.

Until then, we are called to live as citizens and ambassadors of that coming Kingdom. That means seeking justice now because justice will flow from Zion then. It means walking in obedience to God's ways now because his *Torah* will govern the nations then. It means blessing Israel now because she will be the center of God's government then.

The reign from Zion is not just Israel's hope. It is the hope of the whole world. One day, the King will come, the trumpet will sound, and the nations will stream to Jerusalem to worship. Until that day, we keep watch, we bear witness, and we pray: "Your kingdom come, your will be done, on earth as it is in heaven."

"And the LORD will be king over all the earth. On that day the LORD will be one and his name one."
(Zechariah 14:9)

Chapter 13

New Heavens and New Earth: The Consummation of All Things

The reign of Messiah from Zion will bring the world into an age of peace and righteousness unlike anything history has known. Nations will come to Jerusalem to learn God's ways, the land will flourish under his blessing (Isa. 35:1,6-7; Amos 9:13-14), and justice will flow like a river (Amos 5:24). Yet even this will not be the end of the story. At the close of the Millennium, Satan will be released for a short time, leading one final rebellion. This brief rebellion closes the age of restoration and ushers in the consummation of all things. This last act of defiance will be swiftly crushed, and the great judgment before the throne of God will take place (Rev. 20:7-15).

Only then will the new heavens and the new earth appear – the final and eternal reality toward which the whole biblical story has been moving. In this vision, every shadow is gone; the curse that has marked creation since Eden is removed forever (Rom. 8:20-22; Gal. 3:13; Rev. 22:3). Death is no more, pain is no more, and God's presence fills everything.

Revelation 21-22 is the Bible's closing scene, but it is also the culmination of its opening chapters. The story that began in a garden, ends in a garden-like city – Eden renewed, expanded, and glorified. The dwelling place of God is with humanity. Heaven and earth are joined as one. The nations are healed, the Bride is made ready, and God is "all in all" (1 Cor. 15:28). This is not just the end of the Bible. It is the beginning of unending life in the presence of

God. The new Eden is the home we were always meant to have, restored and made new forever.

Eden Renewed, Expanded, and Glorified

John's vision of the new heavens and earth (Rev. 21:1-22:5) is filled with echoes of Genesis 1-2. The Bible's story begins with God creating a good world, placing humanity in a garden to enjoy his presence and extend his reign. It ends with a renewed creation, where God dwells with his redeemed people forever in a garden-like city that shines with his glory.

The parallels are deliberate. In Genesis, a river flows through Eden to water the garden. In Revelation, the river of the water of life flows from the throne of God and of the Lamb, bringing life to the nations (Gen. 2:10; Rev. 22:1-2). In Eden, the tree of life stood at the center, but access to it was lost through sin. In the new creation, the tree of life yields its fruit every month, and its leaves are for the healing of the nations (Gen. 3:22-24; Rev. 22:2). The curse pronounced in Genesis 3 is gone forever: "No longer will there be anything accursed" (Rev. 22:3).[152]

Yet John's vision is not simply Eden restored. It is Eden expanded and glorified. The holy city – the new Jerusalem – comes down out of heaven from God, prepared as a Bride adorned for her Husband (Rev. 21:2). The vision blends imagery of a radiant bride with that of a perfectly crafted city. The city is measured as a perfect cube, directly recalling the proportions of the Most Holy Place in the temple (Rev. 21:16; 1 Kings 6:20), yet profoundly magnified to

---

152 The river and tree of life imagery deliberately echo Genesis 2:9-10 and 3:22-24. In the New Jerusalem, the tree of life is not only restored but is available to all, producing perpetual fruit for the redeemed and bringing healing, which is an image of wholeness for the nations. The removal of the curse (Rev. 22:3) marks the completion of God's redemptive work, ending the exile from Eden and every trace of human alienation from God, creation, and one another.

symbolize God's presence filling all of creation. John records its measurements as 12,000 stadia (approximately 2,220 kilometers / 1,380 miles) on each side. If placed on today's map, this area would cover all the land God promised to Abraham "from the river of Egypt to the great river, the river Euphrates" (Gen. 15:18) – and even more, showing that his presence and blessing will extend to all creation.

In Eden, God walked intimately with humanity in the cool of the day. In the New Jerusalem, "the dwelling place of God is with humanity" (Rev. 21:3) – and nothing will separate his people from his presence. This is the fulfillment of the entire biblical narrative. All Scripture's promises lead to this destination. The prophets envisioned a renewed heaven and earth (Isa. 65:17; 66:22) and a creation overflowing with the knowledge of YHWH (Hab. 2:14). In the New Jerusalem, these hopes are fully realized and infinitely surpassed – what was lost through Adam is abundantly restored in Christ. The garden expands into a radiant city; the sanctuary becomes the whole cosmos; and God's fellowship with his people becomes unbroken and eternal.

The Curse Removed and God's Presence Fully Manifest

One of the most breathtaking statements in John's vision is this: "No longer will there be anything accursed" (Rev. 22:3). With these words, the shadow that has hung over creation since Genesis 3 is finally lifted. In Eden, human rebellion brought a curse upon the ground, pain into human relationships, and death into the human story (Gen. 3:14-19). In the new creation, all of it is gone – not diminished or restrained but removed forever.

This is infinitely more than the absence of sin and rebellion. It is the complete restoration of God's original intent for creation. Isaiah foresaw a day when death would be swallowed up forever.

God would wipe away the tears from every face (Isa. 25:8).[153] Paul described the creation itself groaning under the weight of the curse, longing for the day when it would be "set free from its bondage to corruption" and share in "the freedom of the glory of the children of God" (Rom. 8:21). In the new heavens and new earth, that longing will once and for all be satisfied.

The removal of the curse is inseparably tied to the fullness of God's presence. In the garden, Adam and Eve hid from the LORD because of sin. In the New Jerusalem, nothing will hinder the direct, unbroken fellowship between God and his people. "They will see his face, and his name will be on their foreheads" (Rev. 22:4). This fulfills God's promise to be truly present – with nothing hidden – among his people in a renewed creation.[154]

There will be no temple in the city, "for its temple is the Lord God the Almighty and the Lamb" (Rev. 21:22). The light of God's glory will replace the sun and moon (Rev. 21:23; Isa. 60:19-20). Every trace of separation – physical, spiritual, or symbolic – will be gone. God's presence, which was once localized in the Most Holy Place, will fill all things. His reign will be uncontested, his blessing unbroken, and his people unafraid.

Heaven and Earth United in the Marriage of the Lamb

Revelation 21 opens with a vision of the holy city, the New Jerusalem, "coming down out of heaven from God, prepared as a bride adorned for her husband" (Rev. 21:2). Here, the imagery shifts away from

---

153 Isaiah 25:8 is a prophecy of death's defeat and is linked to the promises fulfilled in Revelation 21-22.

154 The promise of seeing God's face and bearing his name is the climax of covenant relationship. The "name on their foreheads" symbolizes both belonging and consecration: the faithful now enjoy a new status as God's own, fully identified with him, as the divine presence which once dwelled in the temple's Holy of Holies is now shared openly in all of renewed creation.

garden and temple motifs to that of a wedding celebration. The marriage supper of the Lamb, announced in Revelation 19:6-9, served as the formal proclamation that all is ready. In Revelation 21, the ceremony itself is depicted at last: the bride is prepared, the celebration begins, and the covenant relationship is fully realized. The Bridegroom then comes in glory (Rev. 19:11-16), defeats his enemies, and opens the way for this ultimate union and feast to take place.[155]

This sequence mirrors the marriage customs of Second Temple Judaism. A wedding began with the betrothal – a legally binding covenant in which the couple was considered husband and wife, though they did not yet live together. The bride remained in her father's house while the groom prepared a place for her, often in his father's house (cf. John 14:2-3). When the preparations were complete, the groom would set out in a joyous procession, often at night, accompanied by his friends, to bring the bride to the place he had prepared (cf. Matt. 25:1-13). This public arrival marked the pinnacle of anticipation and celebration. Revelation 19:11-16 mirrors this stage, as the Rider on the white horse comes to claim his Bride and establish peace in his Kingdom. Immediately after this came the marriage feast, the public celebration that could last several days (cf. John 2:1-11). In the eschatological vision of Revelation, the marriage supper of the Lamb follows the King's victory, which inaugurates his Messianic reign (Rev. 20:1-6).

---

155 The "marriage supper of the Lamb" in Rev. 19:6-9 is best understood as a proclamation or formal announcement that everything is now ready for the marriage: the Bride has made herself ready and the guests are called blessed. This is not yet the feast itself, but the public, royal summons that all is prepared, in keeping with ancient wedding customs (first the announcement, then the coming and, finally, the celebration). The actual visible coming of the Bridegroom (Messiah) is depicted in Rev. 19:11-16, when he returns in glory, defeats his enemies, and thus inaugurates the conditions for the wedding supper to begin, the final union of Messiah and his people, which is then fully realized in the descent of the New Jerusalem.

Seen this way, there is no thousand-year gap between the marriage ceremony and married life together. The marriage supper inaugurates the age of Messiah's reign. Revelation 19:6-9 announces that the Bride is ready and pronounces blessing on those invited to the feast. In 19:11-16, the Bridegroom arrives in triumph to secure the peace of his realm, clearing the way for the celebration to begin. The marriage supper begins with the inauguration of the Millennium. Revelation 21, then, portrays the same union brought to its full consummation in the new creation, when every enemy – including death itself – has been destroyed.[156]

Throughout Scripture, God's covenant with his people is portrayed in marital terms. Israel is called YHWH's bride, though her unfaithfulness led to exile (Jer. 2:2; Hos. 2:14-20). The prophets looked forward to a day when the covenant relationship would be restored and renewed – when God would rejoice over his people "as the bridegroom rejoices over the bride" (Isa. 62:5).[157] In the New Testament, Paul describes the *ekklesia* as the Bride of Christ, loved, sanctified, and cleansed, "so that he might present the church to himself in splendor" (Eph. 5:25-27).

---

156 The sequential flow of what happens in these chapters in Revelation and the imagery of marriage, procession, and feast in Revelation are not meant to be artificially separated by a literal thousand-year physical gap in "married life." Instead, these are stages of a single, climactic covenant relationship, the announcement, the arrival, the feast, and, ultimately, the full, eternal union. The marriage supper and the subsequent victory of Messiah are part of a single story of consummation. The imagery of the New Jerusalem as the Bride in Rev. 21 signals the final, everlasting fulfillment of this relationship.

157 After periods of unfaithfulness and desolation, Jerusalem (Zion) is no longer forsaken, but "married" (Hebrew: *be 'ulah*), and God takes the role of the rejoicing bridegroom. This metaphor draws on earlier prophetic imagery (e.g., Hosea, Jeremiah), but in Isaiah 62 it is fully positive: God's delight and joy in his people are likened to a husband's joy in his bride. This kind of language expresses most vividly the depth of feeling and unconditional acceptance that characterizes the new relationship which God intends to have with his people. This restoration is both communal (Zion restored) and covenantal (renewed marriage relationship), offering a vision of ultimate reconciliation and joy.

The marriage supper of the Lamb announced in Revelation 19:6-9 is the celebration of this union at Messiah's return and inaugurates the Millennium. In Revelation 21, the wedding imagery reaches its eternal fulfillment. Heaven and earth are now joined. The separation caused by sin is gone, and God's dwelling place is with humanity forever. The union is not temporary or symbolic but the permanent reality of the new creation: "He will dwell with them, and they will be his people, and God himself will be with them as their God" (Rev. 21:3).

Some dispensational teaching has drawn a sharp distinction between "Israel as the wife (or bride) of YHWH" and "the Church as the bride of Christ," as though there were two separate covenant peoples with two different marriages. But in Revelation, there is only one Bride: the redeemed people of God from every tribe, tongue, and nation, which includes the restored remnant of Israel and those redeemed from the nations (Rev. 5:9-10; Eph. 2:11-22). There will not be two brides, but one new man united to the Bridegroom in everlasting covenant love.

This marriage is the final answer to Jesus' prayer in John 17:21-23 – that his people may be one, even as he and the Father are one, and that the love with which the Father has loved the Son may be in them.[158] It is the relationship for which humanity was created, now unbroken and eternal. The marriage of the Lamb is not just a metaphor for joy. It is the reality of God and his people living together in perfect love and unity forever.

---

158 The ultimate answer to Jesus' prayer is realized in the New Jerusalem, when believers experience perfect oneness with God and with each other as the glorified Bride of Messiah. The language and imagery of John 17 point forward to the climactic union and joy of the messianic wedding feast, affirming that the unity, love, and divine indwelling prayed for by Jesus reach their fruition in the marriage celebration at the end of the biblical story.

The Nations Healed, the Bride Made Ready

John's vision of the new creation overflows every boundary. It is not a private hope or a tribal dream, but a cosmic promise that embraces all nations and every corner of the universe. In Revelation 21-22, we see a redeemed humanity drawn from every nation, brought together in the presence of God and the Lamb. The kings of the earth bring their glory into the New Jerusalem (Rev.21:24). The tree of life bears leaves "for the healing of the nations" (Rev. 22:2). This is a direct allusion to Ezekiel's vision of the river flowing from the restored temple, bringing life to the land and healing to the nations: "their leaves were for healing" (Ezek. 47:12). What Ezekiel saw as an end-time temple restoration, John now sees fulfilled in the glorified people of God and God dwelling with humanity.[159]

The nations are no longer defined by rebellion or idolatry but by worship, glory, and restored relationships. Psalm 2 opens with the nations raging and the kings of the earth plotting in vain against YHWH, his Messiah and Zion, the place where he will reign. It is a vivid picture of humanity's corporate resistance to God's rule. Yet the Psalm ends with an invitation: "Serve the LORD with fear… kiss the Son… blessed are all who take refuge in him" (Ps. 2:11-12). Revelation shows the completion of this transformation: the nations that once rebelled now come willingly, bringing their glory into the city and finding healing from the tree of life.

This imagery intentionally reverses the division of Babel (Gen. 11), where human pride divided the nations and scattered humanity. In the restored creation, unity is not achieved by human effort or imperial ambition, but by the redeeming work of the Lamb. The

---

159 Whereas Ezekiel anticipated a rebuilt sanctuary, John sees the prophecy fulfilled in a perfected, worldwide new creation: the city itself is a temple, the people of God are its living stones, and God's unmediated presence fills the redeemed cosmos. The river, now of "the water of life," signifies the outpouring of divine blessing, healing, and immortality, available to all nations. This not only fulfills, but surpasses previous hopes.

unique beauty and honor of every nation are welcomed, not erased, affirming that redeemed cultural and ethnic diversity is woven into the eternal worship of God. The gospel does not erase difference; it purifies and fulfills it, realizing God's ancient promise to bless all peoples through Abraham.

The healing of the nations in Revelation reaches far beyond politics. It transforms individuals and communities alike. First, the Bride is described as clothed in "the righteous deeds of the saints" (Rev. 19:8), and then as "prepared as a bride adorned for her husband" (Rev. 21:2). This readiness is not achieved by human effort but brought about by the Spirit's sanctifying work throughout history. Jew and Gentile, united in Messiah, are purified, shaped, and prepared for eternal union with their King, forming one sanctified people worthy of God's presence.[160]

In this renewed order, we see the full outworking of Ephesians 2:14-16: "He himself is our peace... that he might create in himself one new man in place of the two." What was once a divided humanity is now reconciled – to God and to one another. The nations are no longer rivals or rebels but worshipers. The Bride is no longer fragmented but united. This is the goal of redemption: a healed creation, a sanctified people, and a world filled with the glory of God.

God Is All in All

The story of restoration ends where it began – with God, not only as Creator, but as the radiant presence who now fills all things with unveiled glory. "Then comes the end," writes Paul, "when he delivers

---

160 The "healing of the nations" (Rev. 22:2) is not simply geopolitical or ethnic reconciliation, but includes the gathering, purification, and transformation of individuals and communities – Jew and Gentile together – into a single sanctified Bride, ready for eternal union with her Messiah (see also Revelation chapters 7 and 21).

the kingdom to God the Father… that God may be all in all" (1 Cor. 15:24,28). This is the climax of redemptive history: once Christ has subdued every opposing power, destroyed death, and completed his mediatorial reign, he hands over the perfected Kingdom to the Father. Paul does not view history as a cycle but as a purposeful journey toward its goal – the moment when God's presence fills creation and is fully revealed to all. God will reign unchallenged, as he fills all things with his presence and glory, so that the story returns to and surpasses its beginning. This final vision, "God all in all," is the fulfillment of creation's original purpose, now magnified and made complete through the redeeming work of Messiah. This is not the fading of creation but its transfiguration into glory. It is not creation's end, but its fulfillment.

In the new heavens and new earth, there will be no temple: "for its temple is the Lord God the Almighty and the Lamb" (Rev. 21:22). The city has no need of sun or moon, "for the glory of God gives it light, and its lamp is the Lamb" (Rev. 21:23). These images speak of full and unrestricted access to the presence of God. What once required priests, sacrifices, and sacred architecture is now realized in the all-encompassing presence of God himself.

This is the final answer to every longing in Scripture – for nearness (Exod. 33:18), for restoration (Ps. 126:1), for justice (Amos 5:24), for the resurrection of the dead (Dan. 12:2), and for a love unbroken and eternal (Rom. 8:38-39). The new creation is not merely Eden regained but Eden glorified – a world where death is no more, tears are wiped away, and nothing unclean shall enter (Rev. 21:4,27). It is the union of heaven and earth, the fullness of joy in God's presence, and the unshakable peace of Messiah's eternal reign.

As in the beginning, God again speaks light into the world but now the light never fades. The exile that began east of Eden ends in a city filled with his glory. At last, the prayer of the ages is fulfilled: "Your kingdom come, your will be done, on earth as it is in heaven"

(Matt. 6:10). The dwelling place of God is with humanity. The veil is torn, the curse undone, the exile ended. The former things have passed away. The earth is filled with the knowledge of the LORD as the waters cover the sea. God is all in all.

Pastoral Reflection: Living Toward the New Creation

The hope of the new creation is a promise of renewal for our world – a restoration of this world rather than an escape from this world. It is not the end, but the beginning of all things made right. This future calls us to live purposefully in the present – actively participating as part of God's unfolding story, being prepared as the Bride for the world to come. Heaven and earth will be joined, and God invites us to embody that hope now, showing by our lives what is coming.

To live with this hope means we don't give in to fear or despair. Instead, we live with courage and faith. We plant; we build; we heal; we love. We care for what is broken and live as ambassadors of what is coming. The world is hurting, but we carry hope. We point to the future by how we live in the present. Faithfulness, justice, mercy, and love – these are not small things; they are glimpses of the Kingdom that is coming.

It also means we need to start seeing others differently. We invite people from every nation to become part of God's family because of Jesus' redemptive work on the cross. If kings and nations will one day bring their glory into the New Jerusalem, how can we keep the good news to ourselves? If God will one day dwell with his people forever, how can we settle for shallow faith today? The hope of the new creation calls us to live with devotion, compassion, and purpose.

One day, God will be all in all. The exile will be over. Every tear will be wiped away. Until that day comes, we walk forward, with hope in our hearts and our eyes fixed on the One who is making all things new.

"For behold, I create new heavens
and a new earth,
and the former things shall not be remembered
or come into mind.
But be glad and rejoice forever
in that which I create;
for behold, I create Jerusalem to be a joy,
and her people to be a gladness.
I will rejoice in Jerusalem
and be glad in my people; no more shall be heard
in it the sound of weeping
and the cry of distress."
(Isaiah 65:17-19)

Chapter 14

Becoming a Restorationist Church: Embodying the Story Together

The story of restoration invites us not only to believe it but to embody it. God is forming a people who reflect his purposes: communities rooted in Scripture, alive in the Spirit, and shaped by the hope of the coming Kingdom. The local church, as an expression of the global *ekklesia,* is where this takes visible form. The church is not simply a gathering but a living expression of God's renewal in the world. Each congregation becomes a signpost of what is coming, a dwelling place for God's presence, and a testimony to his faithfulness.

To become a restorationist church is to step into the rhythm of the biblical story: from creation to new creation, from covenant to consummation. It is to build on the foundation laid by the apostles and prophets (Eph. 2:20), to walk in the unity of Jews and Gentiles as "one new man" in Messiah, and to live in anticipation of the Kingdom that is drawing near. When we embrace this calling together, our worship, discipleship, and shared life begin to echo the age to come.

Restoration isn't just an idea. It's a way of life. When churches live this story, they become places of healing and joy, rooted in the Scriptures. They carry the beauty of Israel's hope and the power of Pentecost. They live generously, pray expectantly, and walk together as a family shaped by the promises of God. In every ordinary act of faithfulness, they become what they already are: a people being made ready for the return of the King.

Restoration Begins at Home

Having explored the story of restoration through Scripture, we now turn to its lived expression in the local church. Restoration is not something we wait for at the end of time. It begins now, in the life of the local *ekklesia*. Each congregation is called to be a living signpost of what is coming, a community shaped by the story of God's covenant faithfulness to Israel and the nations. When local churches walk in unity, holiness, and Spirit-empowered love, they become a microcosm of the new creation (2 Cor. 5:17; Rev. 21:1-5). In these communities, the gospel becomes visible. It is not just proclaimed but demonstrated.

Beyond an eschatological vision, restorationist theology is an ecclesiological calling. It calls the Church to recover its identity as a Spirit-filled, Messiah-centered, and Israel-connected people. In the book of Acts, the early Jewish disciples did not stop being Jews when they followed Jesus. Instead, they lived as a renewed remnant within Israel, gathering daily around the apostles' teaching, breaking bread with joy, praying with boldness, and walking in the fear of the Lord (Acts 2:42-47). The Gentile believers who joined them did not replace them but were grafted in, learning to honor the story they had entered (Acts 15; Rom. 11:17-24).

In this way, the local church becomes an outpost – an embassy of the coming restoration, not yet perfect but faithful, not nostalgic for the past but rooted in the ancient story. It is a living sign of what God is doing now, and what he will one day do across the whole earth. Restoration doesn't start in the spotlight or the halls of power. It doesn't begin with big platforms or public events. It begins at tables and in homes, in prayer and in shared meals, in acts of love and lives laid down. It begins with ordinary people who dare to live the extraordinary story together.

Recovering the Apostolic Foundations

A restorationist church is built on something ancient and enduring – grounded not in trends or techniques, but in the faithfulness of God and the story he has told from the beginning. The apostles did not launch a new religion out of innovation or strategy. They bore witness to the fulfillment of Israel's long-awaited hope. Their gospel was rooted in the Hebrew Scriptures and empowered by the Spirit. They declared that the age of restoration had begun and that the crucified Jesus had been raised and enthroned as Israel's Messiah and the world's true Lord (Acts 2:36).

To recover this apostolic foundation is to return to the deep soil from which the early *ekklesia* grew. Paul describes the community of believers as "built on the foundation of the apostles and prophets, Christ Jesus himself being the cornerstone" (Eph. 2:20). This foundation does not represent two disconnected voices, one from Israel's past, the other from the Church's future, but a single, unfolding revelation rooted in Israel's covenants and fulfilled in Messiah. The apostles themselves were Jewish men formed by the Hebrew Scriptures and commissioned by Jesus himself to proclaim God's faithfulness to Israel and the nations.

Restorationism seeks to reclaim the full sweep of the biblical story – from creation to new creation – not as disconnected categories of systematic theology, but as a single, unified narrative. It means honoring the Tanakh as the Church's spiritual inheritance and not merely as background to the gospel. It means seeing the New Testament not as a departure from Israel's Scriptures but as their continuation and fulfillment. When a local church embraces these foundations, it will be rooted in truth, nourished by hope, and aligned with its calling.

If we want our churches to be truly apostolic, we must be rooted in Scripture and empowered by the Holy Spirit, just as the early Church was. The gifts of the Spirit were never meant for personal display but for building up the Body of Messiah and bearing witness to the coming Kingdom. As we restore the foundations of the Church, our goal is not to recreate first-century structures but to embody first-century faithfulness and loyalty: a community centered on Messiah, shaped by Scripture, filled with the Spirit, and sent into the world as a sign of the restoration to come.

Embracing the One New Man Without Erasure

Ephesians 2 declares that in Messiah, God has made "one new man" from Jew and Gentile, not by erasing difference but by reconciling both to God through the cross (Eph. 2:15-16). This unity is not a uniformity. The gospel brings peace by healing hostility, not by flattening identities. The "one new man" is not "one new Gentile" or "one new Jew," but a renewed humanity that reflects God's original intention for creation: a people of every nation reconciled in covenant love.[161]

The Church must resist distortions that threaten the unity and integrity of the Body. Supersessionism, in all its forms, has often silenced or erased Jewish identity within the *ekklesia*. The result is a Church disconnected from its roots, and a gospel stripped of its covenantal context and mission. On the other side, "One Law" movements, though zealous for *Torah*, often burden Gentile believers with requirements that were never intended for them, turning gestures of honor into demands for uniformity.[162] Both errors create confusion and division, and both obscure the beauty of covenantal diversity within the one new man.

---

161 Eph. 2:15-16 describes the creation of "one new man" in place of the divided hostility between Jew and Gentile.

162 See David Rudolph, *One New Man, Hebrew Roots, Replacement Theology*, 7-27, for a critique of 'One Law' approaches that require all believers to keep the same Mosaic commandments and the theological risks of erasing Jewish-Gentile distinction.

Paul's vision of the *ekklesia* honors both shared identity in Messiah and distinct callings within the covenant community (Rom. 11:17-24; 1 Cor. 7:17-20). Jewish believers remain called to live as Jews in continuity with the promises made to their ancestors (Rom. 9:4-5). Gentile believers are grafted in, not as a replacement of Jews but as fellow heirs, called to walk in covenant faithfulness without erasing their own ethnic identity.[163] Together, they form a redeemed community that anticipates the unity of the world to come.

In Ephesians 3:6 Paul describes how Jewish and Gentile believers are joined together in Messiah as "fellow heirs, members of the same body, and partakers of the promise." This foundational reconciliation becomes a model for healing every other ethnic and cultural divide. Ethnic and cultural diversity is not a problem to solve; it is part of the Creator's design. God scattered the nations and fixed their boundaries (Deut. 32:8), and he will one day gather them again before his throne in worship.

The gospel does not erase cultural and ethnic distinctions. It redeems and celebrates them. This stands in stark contrast to ideological systems such as Islam, where religious identity is often closely tied to Arab culture, and believers from other backgrounds are expected to adopt Arabic language, dress, and customs as a sign of their faith. In the Kingdom of God, however, every tribe and tongue is called to worship in the beauty of their God-given distinctiveness. No nation or people group is superior or inferior. The new humanity God is forming is united by shared allegiance to the King and participation in the covenant he fulfills, not by sameness.

---

163 Paul's metaphor of the olive tree in Romans 11 emphasizes both the continuity of Israel's calling and the inclusion of Gentiles without replacement.

Torah and Identity: Loyalty, Not Legalism

Restorationist theology affirms the goodness of *Torah*, not as a system of legalism but as covenantal instruction breathed out by God and fulfilled in Messiah. Under the New Covenant, the law is not abolished but written on human hearts (Jer. 31:33; Heb. 8:10), enabling Spirit-empowered obedience that flows from love rather than obligation.

This means that Jewish and Gentile believers walk in loyalty to the same Lord, though not in identical ways. Jewish followers of Jesus are called to retain their covenantal identity, living as a prophetic sign of Israel's enduring election and future restoration (Rom. 11:1-5). Gentile believers, grafted into the same olive tree by grace through faith, are not required to take on the yoke of the Sinai covenant, but are called to walk in holiness, unity, and love (Acts 15:19-21; Eph. 2:13-22).

Rather than serving as a litmus test for salvation or status, *Torah* – now written on the heart – functions as a transformative framework for discipleship and faithful living, both under the Sinai covenant and now within the New Covenant.[164] As noted earlier, the key difference lies not in the content of the instruction but in its location: *Torah* is now written on hearts, rather than on stone or scrolls.

Torah's deeper purpose is to shape a people who reflect God's character in every sphere of life.[165] The Spirit leads people into

---

164 Under the New Covenant, the *Torah* continues to serve not as a requirement for obtaining salvation but as transformative instruction for the community of faith. This reflects its original purpose under the Sinai covenant, where obedience was a response to God's saving act rather than a prerequisite for it.

165 The *Torah* is foundational for Israel's ethical identity. Its structures and precepts are designed to shape Israel into a community whose life will show what the living God is like. The ethical vision of the *Torah* is linked to the calling of Israel to "be holy as I am holy" (Lev. 19:2). The *Torah's* purpose is deeply tied to reflecting God's moral character in the world, not merely to prescribe rituals or define boundary markers.

covenant faithfulness, not through rule-keeping but through transformed hearts. Legalism imposes burdens. The Spirit brings life. This covenantal obedience does not erase difference. Instead, it honors the distinct callings of Jew and Gentile, male and female, slave and free (Gal. 3:28), without turning their uniqueness into sameness.[166] The goal is harmony, not uniformity. In Messiah, we are "one new man" (Eph. 2:15), not by becoming the same but by being reconciled in our God-given identities. Unity comes through covenantal faithfulness rooted in love, not by conformity.

Worship, Calendar, and Community Practices

Restorationist churches cultivate rhythms of worship and shared life that are rooted in the biblical story and shaped by the Spirit. These rhythms often draw from the richness of the *mo'edim*, God's appointed times – *shabbat* and the feasts of YHWH – which together form the covenant calendar telling the story of redemption from creation to new creation.

For Jewish believers, these practices are not relics of the past but expressions of their ongoing covenant identity. Observing the Sabbath, Passover, *Shavuot*, and *Sukkot* is a way of bearing witness to God's faithfulness and the future hope of Israel's restoration. These rhythms are not legal burdens but acts of worship, remembrance, and prophetic joy.

For Gentile believers, these rhythms are an invitation to honor Israel's story and its fulfillment in Messiah, not a covenant

---

166   When Galatians 3:28 states "neither Jew nor Greek, slave nor free, male and female" it identifies central social divisions of the ancient world but does not call for these distinctions to simply disappear. Instead, Paul's vision is for the Church to be a new kind of community where the particularities of ethnicity, gender, or social status are no longer grounds for exclusion or superiority, even as those differences still exist and can be honored within the Body of Messiah. So, Galatians 3:28 should not be read as erasing individual or group identities. Rather, it establishes a new unity in Messiah that affirms diversity within the community.

requirement. Gentiles are free in the Spirit to worship on Sunday and to celebrate Christ-centered expressions of Easter and Christmas without shame or fear. Claims that these holidays are inherently pagan often rest on uncertain or overstated associations with ancient customs, overlooking how the Church has reoriented these seasons around the life, death, and resurrection of Jesus.[167] Our aim is not to withdraw from the world in fear of contamination but to consecrate our times and seasons to the Lord with wisdom and joy. In fact, during holidays like Easter and Christmas, many non-believers are more open to spiritual conversations than at other times of the year. Rather than avoiding these occasions, we should embrace them as opportunities for meaningful outreach and celebration, filled with a clear and hopeful witness to the gospel of the Kingdom.

Gentile believers are warmly welcomed to join Messianic Jewish communities – and even Jewish communities that do not believe in Messiah Jesus – in celebrating the biblical feasts as a gesture of solidarity and shared hope. This participation is deeply enriched when practiced with humility and respect, avoiding cultural appropriation on one side and pressure toward uniformity on the other. The true beauty of restoration emerges in reciprocal blessing, where diversity is honored rather than erased and each person contributes from their own background and calling.

Rather than enforcing a single model, restorationist communities cultivate Spirit-led creativity in shaping local rhythms of worship, discipleship, rest, hospitality, and joy. Like the early believers who

---

167 For a rebuttal of the claims that Easter was borrowed from a pagan holiday, see Anthony McRoy, "Was Easter Borrowed from a Pagan Holiday?" *The Aquila Report*, April 1, 2018, accessed on Nov. 24, 2025, https://theaquilareport.com/was-easter-borrowed-from-a-pagan-holiday/. For a rebuttal of the pagan roots of Christmas, see Kevin DeYoung, "Is Christmas a Pagan 'Rip-Off'?" The Gospel Coalition, Dec. 15, 2020, accessed on Nov. 25, 2025, https://www.thegospelcoalition.org/blogs/kevin-deyoung/is-christmas-a-pagan-rip-off/.

met daily with glad and sincere hearts (Acts 2:46), they bear witness to the new creation by how they gather, celebrate, and live the story together. These rhythms are not about calendar conformity or rigid alignment with ancient liturgies – whether rooted in Judaism or traditional Christianity – but about faithfully embodying God's redemptive story in time and space. As such, restorationist congregations may take different shapes – some reflecting synagogue patterns, others drawing from historic church liturgies, and still others following more contemporary models found in evangelical, Pentecostal, or charismatic traditions.

Unity and Mission Flow Together

Restoration brings more than theological clarity or renewed practice. It forms a people and a community shaped by love, grace, and truth. The unity of the Body of Messiah is not an optional extra. It is central to the Church's identity and witness. Jesus prayed that his followers would be one, "so that the world may believe" (John 17:21). Paul likewise urged the *ekklesia* to "maintain the unity of the Spirit in the bond of peace," expressing this unity with humility, gentleness, patience, and love (Eph. 4:2-3). This is not a unity that we manufacture for ourselves, but a reality established in Christ through the Spirit. It is a gift we are called to safeguard and embody. Crucially, this unity is not about sameness but covenantal solidarity – a shared life in Messiah that welcomes difference while growing together in maturity.

Such unity reflects the very heart of the gospel. It arises from shared allegiance to Jesus and finds expression in a reconciled community consisting of Jew and Gentile, male and female, slave and free (cf. Gal. 3:28). When the Church embodies this unity, it becomes a signpost for the Kingdom, a foretaste of the age to come. Jesus' words in Matthew 24:14 make the connection clear: "This gospel of the kingdom will be proclaimed throughout the whole world as a testimony to all nations, and then the end will come." The gospel is not only preached. It is demonstrated through a people who live its reality as one new man.

The Great Commission (Matt. 28:18-20) sends the Church into the world to disciple nations, not just to share information but to form communities that reflect the rule of the risen King.[168] This mission is both spoken and lived. Jesus said, "By this all people will know that you are my disciples, if you have love for one another" (John 13:35).[169] Love is not an afterthought – it is the evidence of the gospel.

So, unity and mission belong together in the life of the restorationist church. As Israel and the nations are brought into harmony through Messiah, the Church becomes what it was meant to be: a signpost of the Kingdom and a vessel of God's redeeming love for the world.

What Needs to Be Unlearned?

To become a restorationist church involves more than recovering biblical patterns. It requires the courage to unlearn inherited distortions. Much of Christian tradition has been deeply shaped by supersessionist assumptions – the notion that the Church has

---

168 The Great Commission is a call to replicate the kind of community Jesus formed: shaping culture, values, and way of life, so that the Church becomes an agent of transformation among the nations. True discipleship should involve teaching obedience to all that Jesus commanded (Matt. 28:20), which means nurturing a way of life patterned after the reign of the risen King. This missional vision is communal in scope: the Church is sent to form visible communities that embody and bear witness to God's rule on earth, advancing redemption and reconciliation in every dimension of human existence.

169 Love is the defining and distinguishing mark of discipleship. While doctrinal alignment is essential, Jesus identifies mutual love among believers as the visible and persuasive evidence to the world that they belong to him. Jesus demonstrates this love by washing his disciples' feet earlier in the chapter (John 13:1-17) – an act of self-giving service rooted in the cross. This kind of love is a real-life witness that complements the Church's spoken witness. It is an embodiment of the gospel's truth.

replaced Israel in God's purposes. This mindset has often led to the erasure of Jewish identity within the Body of Messiah and fueled centuries of theological antisemitism, with devastating consequences for both Church and world. True restoration invites the Church to confront these errors honestly, repenting of replacement theology and recovering its rootedness in the promises God made to Israel.

The legacy of supersessionism spans denominations and centuries. Its influence appears in the dogmatic structures and triumphalist theology of the Roman Catholic Church, in the cultural hierarchies of Eastern Orthodoxy, in the doctrine of the Reformers, and in the indifference or ignorance found in much of modern evangelicalism. Restorationist churches must therefore renounce these deeply embedded patterns and return to the Scriptures with renewed humility and openness.

True restoration demands that we face these distortions honestly. Supersessionism is not simply a relic of the past. It lingers in the language, liturgy, and theology of many churches today. Likewise, the shift under Roman emperor Constantine from a persecuted movement to an imperial religion introduced systemic hierarchy, coercion, and cultural dominance – distorting the self-giving, servant character of Jesus and the early apostolic witness.

To walk forward, we must identify and repent of these patterns. The Church must reckon with the ways antisemitism crept into its theology and practice, from the early Fathers through medieval councils to the silence of modern times in the face of Jewish suffering. Restorationist theology insists that Israel still has a role in God's plan and that the Jewish people remain beloved for the sake of the patriarchs. The gospel calls Gentile believers not to arrogance, but to humility, to stand with – not over – the Jewish people (Rom. 11:28).

Unlearning these theological distortions clears the way for genuine reconciliation. It allows the *ekklesia* to become a place where Jews and Gentiles, and people from every nation, can walk together in faithfulness, love, and mutual honor. Restoration cannot move forward without repentance. But when the Church turns from pride and returns to the foundation laid by the apostles and prophets, it becomes again what it was always meant to be: a sign of the world to come. Only then can we, as followers of Jesus, provoke Israel to jealousy (Rom. 11:11), not through coercion, cultural erasure, or triumphalism, but by embodying the covenant love that leads her to her own Messiah.

Restorationist Leadership and Discipleship

Restoration begins with spiritual formation. The local church was never intended to be an audience entertained by ministry professionals, but a family empowered by the Spirit to live the story together. Instead, it is called to be a body, a family, shaped by the Word, empowered by the Spirit, and sent out into the world. Restorationist leadership equips the community to live out this story together, calling believers to be doers of the Word rather than mere consumers of ministry.

Interestingly, the New Testament does not speak much of "leadership" as a role in itself. Instead, it speaks of service, oversight, and shepherding. Apostles, prophets, evangelists, shepherds, teachers, elders, and deacons – these are not hierarchical titles, but functions rooted in care, responsibility, and accountability before the Chief Shepherd (1 Pet. 5:1-4). Leaders in the early Church were not spiritual celebrities or religious executives. They were undershepherds entrusted to guide, guard, and nurture the flock on behalf of Messiah.

This reframes the purpose of leadership: not to gather followers around a personality but to form disciples of Jesus. Restorationist leaders cultivate faithfulness to Jesus, and not to a religious hype. They train people to live out the gospel in everyday life, around tables, in neighborhoods, at work, and in the fellowship of the saints. Their goal is not to build platforms but to build people.

To do this, we must recover a team-based, fivefold model of ministry. Apostles, prophets, evangelists, shepherds, and teachers are given by the ascended Messiah to equip the *ekklesia* and bring it to maturity (Eph. 4:11-13). These gifts are not about control but contribution. They reflect the diverse ways the Spirit builds up the Body for unity and mission. Restorationist churches create space for these gifts to function relationally – not through bureaucracy or limited to Sunday gatherings but woven into a Spirit-empowered communal life.

Discipleship stands at the heart of this vision – not as a matter of gaining information or merely avoiding sin but as a journey of walking alongside others into the unfolding biblical story. True discipleship helps people discover their identity in Messiah and their role in God's mission. Jesus did not commission us to make converts or draw bigger crowds; he called us to make disciples, teaching them to obey all that he had commanded (Matt. 28:20). This obedience is not motivated by fear or obligation, but springs from love – a relational response to the One who gave himself for us.

As the world grows darker and opposition to the gospel increases, authentic discipleship must equip God's people to endure suffering with faith, courage, and hope. Paul reminds us, "All who desire to live a godly life in Christ Jesus will be persecuted" (2 Tim. 3:12). Restorationist discipleship is not about comfort or social influence but about shaping communities able to stand firm in trial, marked by endurance, love, and a steadfast hope that "the one who endures to the end will be saved" (Matt. 24:13). This is not a call to mere survival or pessimism but to apocalyptic hope – a confident expectation that Messiah is coming, the Kingdom will be revealed, and our faithfulness in suffering will not be wasted (Rom. 8:18; Rev. 21:1–5).

Call to Prayer and Prophetic Intercession

A restorationist church is marked by prayer. Its posture is humble and intercessory, not triumphalist. It stands in the gap for a world still groaning under the burden of sin and darkness, refusing to settle for mere fleshly solutions. As Paul writes, "We do not wage war according to the flesh" (2 Cor. 10:3). Our true battle is spiritual. The church's intercession recognizes that our struggle is not against flesh and blood, but against principalities, powers, and cosmic forces of evil in the heavenly realms (Eph. 6:12). Restorationist prayer contends with the ongoing influence of the kingdom of darkness and acknowledges the reality of rebellious spiritual beings – "the gods of the nations" – who will one day be judged (Ps. 82).[170]

Through prayer, the local church participates in heaven's agenda on earth. Intercession lifts our vision beyond personal needs to embrace God's global purposes – moving from momentary relief to the hope of eternal restoration. We pray for the peace of Jerusalem and for Israel's full acceptance of their Messiah (Rom. 11:12,15,26). We intercede for the nations to turn from idols and receive the gospel of the Kingdom. We seek unity in the Body – across cultures, ethnicities, and denominations – because Jesus prayed for it, knowing that our unity is a prophetic witness to the world (John 17:21). We pray for more laborers in the harvest, as Jesus instructed, because the need is great and the workers are few (Matt. 9:37-38). And we yearn for the return of the King, anchoring our hope not in comfort or success but in the glory of his appearing (2 Tim. 4:8).

---

170 Michael S. Heiser, *The Unseen Realm*, esp. 259-260. Heiser explores Psalm 82 as a divine council scene where God pronounces judgment on rebellious *elohim*, linking this to New Testament portrayals of cosmic powers (e.g., Eph. 6:12).

In a time of shaking, prayer is the one thing that anchors the church in hope. It is how we wait with expectation and participate in God's unfolding plan. The call to intercession is not peripheral to restoration. It is at its heart. We do not overcome by clever strategies or persuasive words but by abiding in Christ and lifting our voices in prayer. The great revivals of history were birthed in prayer rooms, not in boardrooms.

To be a praying church is to resist apathy, distraction, and defeatism. The Spirit still speaks, still groans, still moves, and still intercedes (Rom. 8:26-27). A restorationist church listens to the Spirit and joins in that groaning. It weeps for what is broken and waits and labors in hope for its restoration.

Pastoral Reflection: A Church Ready for Dark and Glorious Days Ahead

The call to become a restorationist church is not merely about reclaiming ancient truths or refining ministry methods. It is about becoming a people ready for the return of the King. We are more than stewards of a message. We are participants in a story that is rushing toward its appointed climax. The days ahead will not be easy. Scripture warns that before the renewal of all things, deception, trials, and suffering will increase. We are entering a time of shaking.

As Hebrews declares, "This phrase, 'Yet once more,' indicates the removal of things that are shaken – that is, things that have been made – in order that the things that cannot be shaken may remain" (Heb. 12:27). Everything that can be shaken will be shaken – and that shaking has already begun. Cultural idols are toppling, compromised structures are being exposed, and shallow faith is collapsing. In this hour, God is purifying his people, so that only what is firmly rooted in him – a life founded on the King and his Kingdom – will endure.

This shaking also marks the downfall of celebrity-driven Christianity. The era of "celebrity Christianity" is coming to an end, as God dismantles every pedestal and exposes the folly of fame-based platforms. We were never called to follow "great men of God" but to follow the crucified and risen Messiah. Our task is not to chase influence or popularity but to cultivate communities of faithfulness. Restorationist churches must reject the spectacle and recover the beauty of simplicity: shared life, sacrificial love, and a Spirit-empowered witness.

This is not a time for fear. It is a time for clarity; a time for urgency; a time to live the gospel with eyes fixed on Jesus and hearts burning for his return. If persecution comes – and it will – we must be ready. If deception increases – and it already has – we must be grounded. If the cost of faithfulness rises – and it surely will – we must not waver. So, we do not lose heart. We keep building. We keep loving. We keep watching and praying. Restoration is not just a future event. It is a present calling. A people shaped by this story will live differently; and when the shaking comes, they will not be moved.

The Spirit is once again saying to the churches: Repent. Return. Remember who you are. Remember whose you are. Now put your hand to the plow and prepare the way for the Lord!

"Be watchful, stand firm in the faith,
act like men, be strong.
Let all that you do be done in love."
(1 Corinthians 16:13-14)

Chapter 15

The Story That Shapes Our Mission

The restoration story that began in Eden moves toward its climax in mission – a people renewed by grace and sent to prepare the earth for the King's return. The *ekklesia*'s mission rises from that same divine narrative of creation, covenant, and redemption: the unfolding drama of God's covenant faithfulness, fulfilled in Messiah and pressing toward the renewal of all things. This story is the pulse of our hope and the pattern of our calling. To live as a restorationist community is to be continually shaped by this divine rhythm: creation, covenant, exile, return, redemption, and new creation. The gospel is far more than a promise of personal salvation. It is the royal announcement that Israel's story finds its fulfillment in Jesus and is now advancing to the ends of the earth.

This is the story that gives us our identity. It tells us who we are and anchors us to where we are heading. We are the people of the risen King – living in the sacred space between Jesus' resurrection and his return, carrying the presence of the age to come into a world that is passing away. God's mission is not an add-on to church life. It is the very heartbeat of our existence. We are called to stand as a sign and a foretaste of the Kingdom that is coming soon.

We embody this story by living a way of life that stands apart – no longer conformed to the patterns of this world but continually transformed by the renewing of our minds (Rom. 12:2). We carry the fragrance of the age to come into a world weighed down by the burden of sin and rebellion. Our covenant faithfulness is not an attempt to earn salvation, but a sign that we are already part of the unfolding story God is writing in our midst. Our lives become living parables, pointing forward to the restoration that awaits on the horizon.

Living within this story compels us to reject the secular illusion that history is random or aimless. Biblical hope is not naïve optimism but a deep, unwavering confidence that God is faithful to his promises and will guide history toward its appointed goal. This hope shapes the way we love, persevere, and serve. It gives us courage not to lose heart even as the world around us grows darker. Instead, we keep planting gardens, raising families, making disciples, seeking justice, and praying for revival, knowing that restoration is something we embody, not merely proclaim. For, as Scripture reminds us, "we are his workmanship, created in Christ Jesus for good works, which God prepared beforehand, that we should walk in them" (Eph. 2:10). We are living witnesses to the story of new creation breaking into the present.

The Dual Calling: To Israel and to the Nations

The restoration story calls the Church to embrace a twofold mission: to provoke Israel to jealousy and to proclaim the gospel to the nations. These are not competing tasks, but two aspects of the same divine calling (Rom. 11:11-14). The worldwide ingathering of Gentiles will reach its fullness, after which Israel's full inclusion will bring resurrection life to whole the world (Rom. 11:15,25-26).[171]

Israel is stirred to jealousy as she witnesses Gentiles openly serving the God of Israel, embracing the covenant blessings once given uniquely to her. This awakening arises not only from

---

171 Paul links Israel's restoration with global blessing. The temporary hardness affecting Israel serves a divine purpose: allowing Gentiles to come into the family of faith, which in turn will provoke Israel to jealousy, which will lead to their recognition of Messiah and their restoration. When Israel's "full inclusion" occurs, it will have eschatological, life-giving consequences for all humanity, as Paul puts it: "What will their acceptance mean? It will be life from the dead!"

witnessing the joy of the Gentiles but also from seeing these former outsiders now honor and follow Israel's God as their own, stirring in Israel a renewed longing to return to her God. According to Romans, God uses this longing to help guide Israel back to faith, making them desire what is rightly theirs once more.[172]

As Israel's heart is stirred and prepared for spiritual restoration, God's promise is also for every people, tribe, and tongue. The resurrection of Jesus demonstrates his Lordship over all (Acts 10:36), and the Church is commissioned to disciple every nation (Matt. 28:19). Their mission is not about imposing uniformity or erasing the richness of diverse cultures but about inviting each people group into God's family. A restorationist vision honors the distinct gifts and beauty of every culture, while calling all into covenant loyalty to Israel's Messiah.[173]

These two callings – to Israel and the nations – form one redemptive mission. The promise to Abraham was always meant to extend outward: "In you all the families of the earth shall be blessed" (Gen. 12:3). God's faithfulness to Israel is the guarantee of his faithfulness to the rest of the world. And the fullness of the Gentiles leads to Israel's salvation, so that God's mercy might overflow to all (Rom. 11:25-32). There is a mysterious beauty in this divine dance – Israel and the nations moving together, each responding to God's

---

172 The "jealousy" in Romans 11 is a positive, covenantal longing. When we provoke Israel to jealousy we invite Israel into a joyful recognition of the covenant's realization, seen in the vibrant life and witness of the *ekklesia* (Church). The Church's role is to awaken a desire for deeper relationship with God, not apply hostile pressure or shame. The proper attitude toward Israel is one of honor, humility, and love: Gentile followers of Jesus are called to reflect the Spirit-filled, Messiah-centered life that embodies Israel's destiny in its truest form, in the hope that this will draw Israel toward her Messiah.

173 Biblical mission affirms cultural diversity while calling all nations to worship the one true God. The call to disciple all the nations (Matt. 28:19) is not a mandate for cultural imperialism or erasing ethnic identity. Instead, it is an invitation for every people and culture to bring their unique "glory" into the worship of the one true God (cf. Rev. 21:24-26).

faithfulness, until all are caught up in the fullness of his mercy and blessing.

Spirit-Filled Witness and the Gospel of the Kingdom

The restoration story is more than a message; it is a living reality. The gospel of the Kingdom bursts into our world with the wind and fire of the Spirit – shattering chains, opening blind eyes, and lifting the broken from the dust (Luke 4:18-19). Kingdom witness is not only spoken; it is demonstrated through miracles, healings, deliverance, and acts of mercy, each serving as a signpost of the world to come – lightning on the horizon, stirring holy hope, and inviting the weary to repentance and faith in Messiah.[174] Word and deed belong together – the message of the Kingdom is authenticated by the work of the Spirit.

This pattern is witnessed through the ministry of Jesus and the apostles: the Kingdom is proclaimed with clarity and made real in tangible power (Matt. 9:35; Acts 8:6-8). As the *ekklesia* walks in this same Spirit, it partakes of the "powers of the age to come" (Heb. 6:5), bearing living witness to the restoration promised in Scripture.[175] Our calling is not just to announce God's reign but to embody it in love, justice, and supernatural healing.

When the nations behold the people of God united, holy, and filled with the Spirit's power, the gospel rises above mere words.

---

174 Jesus' healings were not random acts of compassion alone, but prophetic acts announcing the inbreaking reign of God.

175 The phrase "powers of the age to come" in Hebrews 6:5 reflects the Jewish apocalyptic expectation that the Messianic Age of restoration would be marked by supernatural renewal. In Second Temple Jewish thought, history was divided into "this age" (*olam hazeh*) and "the age to come" (*olam habba*), anticipating that God's power – seen in healing, deliverance, and spiritual renewal – would break into the present. An explanation of *olam hazeh* and *olam habba* from an orthodox Jewish perspective can be found in Zalman Goldstein, "Introduction: The Journey of Life," *Chabad. org*, accessed November 24, 2025, https://www.chabad.org/library/article_cdo/aid/364281/jewish/Intro-The-Journey-of-Life.htm.

It becomes a visible sign, pointing toward the day the King will return, the dead will be raised, and creation will be renewed.[176]

Hastening the Day: Unity and Proclamation

Peter's words should awaken us: "Since all these things are thus to be dissolved, what sort of people ought you to be in lives of holiness and godliness, waiting for and hastening the coming of the day of God..." (2 Peter 3:11-12). Holiness and mission are not competing paths but the heartbeat of Peter's vision. Holiness breathes the fragrance of the coming Kingdom into our lives. Mission carries that fragrance to the very streets and corners of the world. When God's people are set apart for him, their lives become a living answer to Peter's challenge – a visible sign of another age, where hope and renewal fill the air. A restorationist church does not separate being called out from being sent. It holds them together, set apart for God and sent into the world so that his promises go forth in power and beauty.

We hasten the day of the Lord by pursuing **unity and** through Spirit-filled proclamation. Unity is not a side project, but a prophetic sign of the Kingdom. Jesus prayed for this unity so that the world would believe (John 17:21), and Paul called the *ekklesia* to guard it with humility, gentleness, patience, and love (Eph. 4:2-3). When Jew and Gentile, male and female, every tribe and tongue walk together in covenantal solidarity, we give the world – and even the principalities and powers in the heavenly realms (Eph. 3:10) – a glimpse of God's final purpose for creation.

Proclamation flows from this unity like a river. The gospel of the Kingdom will be proclaimed to all nations, "and then the end will come" (Matt. 24:14). This is not a timeline to watch passively, but a

---

176 On the unity and holiness of the Church as a visible witness to the coming Kingdom, see John 17:20-23; Eph. 4:1-6.

commission to embrace urgently. The *ekklesia* is sent to announce the reign of Jesus in word and deed – confronting darkness, healing the hurting, and setting captives free (Luke 4:18-19). Miracles, healings, and acts of mercy are prophetic signs, revealing in the present what God has promised to do for all creation when Messiah returns.

As the gospel is being proclaimed to the ends of the earth, the Spirit uses the ingathering of Gentiles to provoke Israel to jealousy, awakening her to recognize Jesus as her Messiah and return to the God of her ancestors. This turning will lead to Israel's full inclusion, which Scripture says will mean "life from the dead" for the world (Rom. 11:12, 15, 26). Unity, proclamation, and the salvation of Israel are not separate threads but interwoven strands of the one story God is bringing to its appointed climax.

To live this way is to arrange everything – our lives, churches and families – around the return of the King. It is to long for his appearing, to cry with the Spirit and the Bride, "Maranatha!" and to labor until the earth is filled with the knowledge of his glory as the waters cover the sea (Hab. 2:14). This is our holy urgency: to love until he comes, to work until he reigns in Zion, and to stand ready when the trumpet sounds.

Pastoral Reflection: Living the Story Until He Comes

We live in the middle of God's great story – creation, covenant, redemption, and restoration. The King has come, the Spirit has been poured out, and the gospel is going forth to the ends of the earth. Yet the story is still moving toward its climax: the King's return, the salvation of Israel and the renewal of all things.

The days ahead will bring shaking. As Hebrews declares, "This phrase, 'Yet once more,' indicates the removal of things that are shaken – that is, things that have been made – in order that the things that cannot be shaken may remain." (Heb. 12:27). What is built on pride, celebrity, or shallow faith will collapse. What is rooted in the Kingdom will stand.

In such a time, the Church cannot settle for comfort or distraction. We belong to the age to come, even as we live in this present age. We are the people between the resurrection and the return, a people formed by the Word, filled with the Spirit, and focused on the day when the King appears.

So, we keep building. We keep loving. We keep proclaiming the gospel of the Kingdom. We keep working for Jerusalem's peace, for the nations' harvest, and for the unity of the Body. We plant gardens in exile, raise families in hope, serve the poor, and heal the brokenhearted. We walk in holiness, knowing that what we do in the present will echo in eternity in the new creation.

Our eyes are fixed on that day when the trumpet sounds and the heavens open. On that day, the One who was pierced will be seen, and all creation will be restored. This is our hope: the joy of seeing the Bridegroom face to face. Until that day, we prepare the way. We stand as watchmen on the walls, crying out for the return of the King. And so, we pray: "Come, Lord Jesus. *Maranatha.*"

"And I heard a loud voice from the throne saying,
"Behold, the dwelling place of God is with man.
He will dwell with them,
and they will be his people,
and God himself will be with them as their God.
He will wipe away every tear from their eyes,
and death shall be no more,
neither shall there be mourning,
nor crying, nor pain anymore, for the former
things have passed away.
... And he who was seated on the throne said,
Behold, I am making all things new... It is done!
I am the Alpha and the Omega,
the beginning and the end.
To the thirsty I will give from the spring of the
water of life without payment. The one who
conquers will have this heritage,
and I will be his God and he will be my son."

(Revelation 21:3-7)

Bibliography

Adu-Ntow, Richard. "Messiah in the Feast of First Fruits." *Jacob's Ladder Christian Fellowship.* https://www.jacobsladdercf. org.uk/teaching-articles/feast-of-first-fruits/messiah-in-the-feast-of-first-fruits. Accessed on Sept. 23, 2025.

Alexander, T. Desmond. *From Eden to the New Jerusalem: An Introduction to Biblical Theology.* Grand Rapids, MI Kregel, 2008.

Athelstan Scalzo, Francis-David. *The Jewish Basis for the Born Again Experience in John 3.* A Dissertation Submitted to the Faculty of the John W. Rawlings School of Divinity in Lynchburg, VA, 2022.

Bates, Matthew, *Salvation by Allegiance Alone.* Grand Rapids, MI: Baker Academic, 2017.

Beale, Gregory K. *A New Testament Biblical Theology.* Grand Rapids, MI: Baker Academic, 2011.

Ben-Dov, Meir. *In the Shadow of the Temple.* New York: HarperCollins, 1985.

Block, Daniel I. *The Gods of the Nations: Studies in Ancient Near Eastern National Theology.* Grand Rapids, MI: Baker Academic, 2001.

Blumenthal, Ariel Laurence. *One New Man: Reconciling Jew & Gentile in One Body of Christ.* Sisters, OR: Deep River Books, 2018.

Chen, Kevin S. *The Messianic Vision of the Pentateuch: A Biblical-Theological Introduction to the Messiah and His People.* Downers Grove, IL: IVP Academic, 2019.

Collins, C. John. *Genesis 1-4: A Linguistic, Literary, and Theological Commentary.* Phillipsburg, NJ: P&R Publishing, 2006.

Cook, Stephen L. "The Temple in the Christian Bible." *St Andrews Encyclopaedia of Theology*, Aug. 10, 2023. https://www. saet.ac.uk/Christianity/TheTempleintheChristianBible. Accessed on Nov. 21, 2025.

Currid, John D. *Against the Gods: The Polemical Theology of the Old Testament*. Wheaton, IL: Crossway, 2013.

Damgaard, Finn. "Propaganda Against Propaganda: Revisiting Eusebius' Use of the Figure of Moses in the *Life of Constantine*." In *Eusebius of Caesarea: Tradition and Innovations*. Edited by Aaron P. Johnson and Jeremy Schott. Washington, DC: Center for Hellenic Studies, 2013. https://chs.harvard.edu/chapter/6-propaganda-against-propaganda-revisiting-eusebius-use-of-the-figure-of-moses-in-the-life-of-constantine-finn-damgaard/. Accessed on Nov. 23, 2025.

Dauermann, Stuart. "An Inconvenient Truth: A Right Understanding of the One New Man." *Interfaithfulness*. https://interfaithfulness.org/an-inconvenient-truth-a-right-understanding-of-the-one-new-man/. Accessed on Aug. 26, 2025.

DeYoung, Kevin. "Is Christmas a Pagan 'Rip-Off'?" *The Gospel Coalition*, Dec.15, 2020. https://www.thegospelcoalition. org/blogs/kevin-deyoung/is-christmas-a-pagan-rip-off/. Accessed on Nov. 25, 2025.

Dunn, James D. G. *The Theology of Paul the Apostle*. Grand Rapids, MI: Eerdmans, 1998.

Dunn, James D. G. *The New Perspective on Paul*, revised ed. Grand Rapids, MI: Eerdmans, 2008.

Eames, Christopher. "The Temple Warning Inscriptions: 'Closest Thing to the Temple We Have.'" *Armstrong Institute of Biblical Archaeology*, Aug. 1, 2021. https://www.armstronginstitute.

org/360-the-temple-warning-inscriptions-closest-thing-to-the-temple-we-have. Accessed on Nov. 24, 2025.

Estelle, Bryan D. "The Exodus Motif in the Christian Bible." *St Andrews Encyclopaedia of Theology*, Nov. 2023. https://www.saet.ac.uk/Christianity/TheExodusMotifintheChristianBible. Accessed on Nov. 21, 2025.

Fee, Gordon D. *The First Epistle to the Corinthians.* New International Commentary on the New Testament. Grand Rapids, MI: Eerdmans, 1987.

Frostad, Ben. "Spirit in Judaism – Part 1: Second Temple Era." *Segullah*, Oct. 27, 2017. https://www.segullah.net/spirit-judaism-part-1/. Accessed on Nov. 22, 2025.

Goldstein, Zalman. "Introduction: The Journey of Life." *Chabad.org*. https://www.chabad.org/library/article_cdo/aid/364281/jewish/Intro-The-Journey-of-Life.htm. Accessed on Nov. 25, 2025.

Hahn, Scott. W. *Kinship by Covenant: A Canonical Approach to the Fulfillment of God's Saving Promises.* New Haven, CT: Yale University Press, 2009.

Havenar, Anna Beth. "Repairing a Broken World: The Jewish Concept of Tikkun Olam." *Light of Messiah Ministries Blog*, Feb. 6, 2024. https://lightofmessiah.org/blog/repairing-a-broken-world-the-jewish-concept-of-tikkun-olam. Accessed on Nov. 21, 2025.

Heiser, Michael S. *The Unseen Realm: Recovering the Supernatural Worldview of the Bible.* Bellingham, WA: Lexham Press, 2015.

Heiser, Michael. "Two Powers in Heaven." https://drmsh.com/the-naked-bible/two-powers-in-heaven/. Accessed on July 9, 2025.

Hubbard, David Allan. *Joel and Amos*. Tyndale Old Testament Commentaries, vol. 25. Downers Grove, IL: IVP Academic, 2009.

Imes, Carmen Joy. *Bearing Yhwh's Name at Sinai: A Reexamination of the Name Command of the Decalogue*. University Park, PA: Eisenbrauns, 2018.

Imes, Carmen Joy. *Bearing God's Name: Why Sinai Still Matters*. Downers Grove, IL: IVP Academic, 2019.

Instone-Brewer, David. "What Did Jesus Mean by 'Three Days and Three Nights'?" *Associates for Biblical Research*, Feb. 21, 2024. https://biblearchaeology.org/abr-projects/the-daniel-9-24-27-project-2/5134-what-did-jesus-mean-by-three-days-and-three-nights. Accessed on Aug. 21, 2025.

Juster, Daniel C. & Intrater, Keith (Asher). *Israel, the Church, and the Last Days*. Shippensburg, PA: Destiny Image Publishers, 2003.

Keener, Craig S. *Acts: An Exegetical Commentary*, vol. 3. Grand Rapids, MI: Baker Academic, 2014.

Keener, Craig S. "Gospel, Good News." *St Andrews Encyclopaedia of Theology*, June 25, 2023. https://www.saet.ac.uk/Christianity/GospelGoodNews. Accessed on July 9, 2025.

Kennedy, Jeff. "Is Jesus the Messianic Davidide of Psalm 2?" *Christotelic Faith*. https://www.christotelic.faith/articles/is-jesus-the-messianic-davidide-of-psalm-2. Accessed on July 10, 2025.

Kinzer, Mark S. *Postmissionary Messianic Judaism: Redefining Christian Engagement with the Jewish People*. Grand Rapids, MI: Baker Academic, 2005.

Ladd, George Eldon. *The Presence of the Future: The Eschatology of Biblical Realism*. Grand Rapids, MI: Eerdmans, 1974.

Lendering, Jona. "Qumran's Dual Messianism." *Livius.org*, 2001. https://www.livius.org/articles/religion/messiah/messiah-9-two-messiahs/. Accessed on Nov. 22, 2025.

Levenson, Jon D. *Resurrection and the Restoration of Israel – The Ultimate Victory of the God of Life.* New Haven, CT: Yale University Press, 2006.

Lizorkin-Eyzenberg, Eli. *The Jewish Gospel of John: Discovering Jesus, King of All Israel.* Self-published, 2019.

Mace, James T. *Ensign for the Nations: The Heilsgeschichtlicher Phase of Messianic Reunification in Luke–Acts.* M.Litt. thesis, University of St. Andrews, 2012.

McRoy, Anthony. "Was Easter Borrowed from a Pagan Holiday?" *The Aquila Report.* April 1, 2018. https://theaquilareport.com/was-easter-borrowed-from-a-pagan-holiday/. Accessed on Nov. 24, 2025.

Moen, Skip. "The Church." May 10, 2009. https://skipmoen.com/2009/05/the-church/. Accessed on July 10, 2025.

Morales, L. Michael. *The Tabernacle Pre-Figured: Cosmic Mountain Ideology in Genesis and Exodus.* PhD diss., University of Bristol / Trinity College, May 9, 2011.

Morales, L. Michael. *Who Shall Ascend the Mountain of the Lord?* Downers Grove, IL: IVP Academic, 2015.

Philpot, Josh. "What 'Taking the Lord's Name in Vain' Really Means – Review: 'Bearing God's Name: Why Sinai Still Matters' by Carmen Joy Imes." *The Gospel Coalition US Edition,* Sept. 21, 2020. https://www.thegospelcoalition.org/reviews/bearing-god-name-sinai-carmen-joy-imes/. Accessed on July 12, 2025.

Prince, Derek. "Aligning Ourselves with Israel." Podcast audio. Derek Prince Ministries. https://www.derekprince.com/radio/145. Accessed on Sept. 20, 2025.

Reed, Annette Yoshiko. *Jewish–Christianity and the History of Judaism*. Tübingen: Mohr Siebeck, 2018.

Richardson, Joel. *When a Jew Rules the World*. Leawood, KS: WinePress Media, 2015.

Rillera, Andrew R. "Tertium Genus or Dyadic Unity? Investigating Sociopolitical Salvation in Ephesians." *Biblical Research* 66 (2021): 31-51. https://digitalcommons.georgefox.edu/cgi/viewcontent.cgi?article=1061&context=dmin. Accessed on November 23, 2025.

Rowland, Christopher, and Christopher R. A. Morray-Jones. *The Mystery of God: Early Jewish Mysticism and the New Testament*. Compendia Rerum Iudaicarum ad Novum Testamentum 12. Leiden: Brill, 2009.

Rudolph, David. *One New Man, Hebrew Roots, Replacement Theology: How to Restore the Jewish Roots of the Christian Faith Without Getting Weird*. Southlake, TX: The King's University, Sept. 8, 2021. https://collective.tku.edu/wp-content/uploads/2021/09/One-New-Man-Hebrew-Roots-Replacement-Theology.pdf. Accessed on July 13, 2025.

Sanders, E. P. *Paul and Palestinian Judaism*. Philadelphia: Fortress Press, 1977.

Segal, Alan F. *Two Powers in Heaven: Early Rabbinic Reports About Christianity and Gnosticism*. Leiden: Brill Academic Publishers, 2002.

"Shavuot History." *Reform Judaism*. https://reformjudaism.org/jewish-holidays/shavuot/shavuot-history. Accessed on July 13, 2025.

Showers, Renald. "A Description and Early History of Millennial Views." *Israel My Glory*, June/July 1986. https://israelmyglory.org/article/a-description-and-early-history-of-millennial-views. Accessed on Nov. 24, 2025.

Soulen, R. Kendall. *The God of Israel and Christian Theology*. Minneapolis: Fortress, 1996.

Stander, Reinhardt. *Preterism, Futurism or Historicism? A Theological Analysis of Three Interpretive Schools of Apocalyptic Prophecy within the Doctrine of the Last Things*. PhD diss., Stellenbosch University, 2021. https:// scholar.sun.ac.za/server/api/core/bitstreams/d24074e1-fbcb-457a-9703-6b27afaf01b2/content. Accessed on Nov. 24, 2025.

Steigmann-Gall, Richard. *The Holy Reich: Nazi Conceptions of Christianity, 1919-1945*. Cambridge: Cambridge University Press, 2003.

Stern, David H. *Jewish New Testament Commentary*. Revised edition. Clarksville, MD: Lederer Books, 2023.

Stern, David H. *Restoring the Jewishness of the Gospel*. Clarksville, MD: Messianic Jewish Publishers, 2010.

Turner, Joe. "Feast of First Fruits." *EZTorah*. https://eztorah.com/ archive/feast-of-first-fruits/. Accessed on Sept. 23, 2025.

Van Dorn, Doug. *The Angel of the LORD: A Biblical, Historical, and Theological Study*. Erie, CO: Waters of Creation, 2020.

Wenham, Gordon J. "Sanctuary Symbolism in the Garden of Eden Story." In *Proceedings of the Ninth World Congress of Jewish Studies*. Jerusalem: World Union of Jewish Studies, 1986.

Williamson, Paul R. *Sealed with an* Oath*: Covenant in God's Unfolding Purpose*. Downers Grove, IL: IVP Academic, 2007.

Winberg, Seth. "Aleinu." *My Jewish Learning*. https://www. myjewishlearning.com/article/aleinu/. Accessed on Aug. 6, 2025.

World Jewish Congress. "Why Anti-Zionism Is a Form of Antisemitism." World Jewish Congress. https://www.

worldjewishcongress.org/en/anti-zionism. Accessed on November 27, 2025.

Wright, N.T. *The New Testament and the People of God.* Minneapolis: Fortress Press, 1992.

Wright, N. T. "Early Traditions and the Origins of Christianity." *Sewanee Theological Review* 41, no. 2 (1998). Reprinted online at N. T. Wright Online, April 5, 2016. https://ntwrightpage.com/2016/04/05/early-traditions-and-the-origins-of-christianity/. Accessed on July 12, 2025.

Wright, N.T. *Surprised by Hope: Rethinking Heaven, the Resurrection, and the Mission of the Church.* New York: HarperOne, 2008.

Primary works

Biblical Texts and Related Editions

The Holy Bible: English Standard Version. Wheaton, IL: Crossway Bibles, 2016.

Biblia Hebraica Stuttgartensia. Edited by Karl Elliger and Wilhelm Rudolph. Stuttgart: Deutsche Bibelgesellschaft, 1997.

Tanakh: The Holy Scriptures. Philadelphia: Jewish Publication Society, 1985.

Septuaginta: id est Vetus Testamentum graece iuxta LXX interpretes. Edited by Alfred Rahlfs. Stuttgart: Deutsche Bibelgesellschaft, 1979.

The Dead Sea Scrolls: Study Edition. Ed. Florentino García Martínez, Eibert J. C. Tigchelaar. Leiden: Brill, 1997.

The Greek New Testament. 5th ed. Ed. Barbara Aland, et al. Stuttgart: Deutsche Bibelgesellschaft, 2014.

Apocrypha and Second Temple Literature

1 Enoch. In *The Old Testament Pseudepigrapha*, vol. 1. Ed. James H. Charlesworth. New York: Doubleday, 1983.

Jubilees. In *The Old Testament Pseudepigrapha*, vol. 2. Ed. James H. Charlesworth. New York: Doubleday, 1985.

Philo of Alexandria. *The Works of Philo: Complete and Unabridged*. Translated by C. D. Yonge. Peabody, MA: Hendrickson Publishers, 1993.

Psalms of Solomon. In *The Old Testament Pseudepigrapha*, vol. 2. Ed. James H. Charlesworth. New York: Doubleday, 1985.

Rabbinic and Early Jewish Texts

lmud. Translated by Isidore Epstein. London: Soncino Press, 1935-1952.

ld Friedlander. London: Kegan Paul, Trench, Trübner & Co., 1916. https://www.sefaria.org/Pirkei_DeRabbi_Eliezer. Accessed on July 8, 2025.

Targum Jonathan on Ezekiel 37:25. Sefaria. https://www.sefaria. org/Ezekiel.37.25. Accessed on July 10, 2025.

Church Fathers and Early Christian Texts

Chrysostom, John. "Discourses Against Judaizing Christians." In *The Fathers of the Church*, Vol. 68. Translated by Paul W. Harkins. Washington, DC: Catholic University of America Press, 1979.

Council of Laodicea. "Canons of the Council of Laodicea." In *Nicene and Post-Nicene Fathers*, Series 2, Vol. 14, edited by Philip Schaff and Henry Wace. Grand Rapids, MI: Eerdmans, 1956.

Eusebius of Caesarea. *Life of Constantine*. Translated by Averil Cameron and Stuart G. Hall. Oxford: Clarendon Press, 1999.

Ignatius of Antioch. "Letter to the Magnesians." In *The Apostolic Fathers: Greek Texts and English Translations*, edited and translated by Michael W. Holmes, 3e ed. Grand Rapids, MI: Baker Academic, 2007.

Ignatius of Antioch. "Letter to the Philadelphians." In *The Apostolic Fathers: Greek Texts and English Translations*, edited and translated by Michael W. Holmes, 3e ed. Grand Rapids, MI: Baker Academic, 2007.

Irenaeus. *Against Heresies.* In The Ante-Nicene Fathers, vol. 1. Ed. Alexander Roberts, James Donaldson. Peabody, MA: Hendrickson Publishers, 1994.

Justin Martyr. *Dialogue with Trypho*. In The Ante-Nicene Fathers, vol. 1. Ed. Alexander Roberts, James Donaldson. Peabody, MA: Hendrickson Publishers, 1994.

Melito of Sardis. *On the Pascha*. Translated with introduction and notes by Alistair Stewart-Sykes. Popular Patristics Series 16. Crestwood, NY: St. Vladimir's Seminary Press, 2001.

Origen. On *First Principles*. Translated and annotated by G. W. Butterworth. Gloucester, MA: Peter Smith, 1973.

Tertullian. *Apology*. In The Ante-Nicene Fathers, vol. 3. Ed. Alexander Roberts, James Donaldson. Peabody, MA: Hendrickson Publishers, 1994.

Modern Hebrew and Rabbinic References (via Digital Collections)

Hebrew Bible – TANAKH and related rabbinic commentary (Targum Onkelos, Rashi, Ramban), per citations accessed via Sefaria.org. Last accessed on 9 August 2025.